Take Five A Day CARS Everything Year by Year Open 1:55 Series Collector's Guide 2006 to 2017 copyright © 2018 by TakeFiveADay.com

Written & Photographed by "KC"

Special Thanks to Samuel K. & David V.

TakeFiveADay.com Co-Founders: "KC" & "MT"

Be sure & visit us everyday on the web for all the fun pop culture news.

MATTEL DISNEY PIXAR CARS | YEAR BY YEAR CHECKLIST
INTRODUCTION

This checklist shows each CARS 1 through CARS 3 character in its original series of year release - earlier years have gaps so they are broken down by wave also. Within each year or wave, the CARS characters are listed alphabetically. While it is in theory possible to list them in order of actual release, it's not necessarily accurate anyway as different cases arrive at different stores shelves and Mattel will sometimes release a case with a "higher" code first so the design motif, wave or year are just as accurate. Rubber tire racers are listed by their wave. Expanded Universe releases are grouped by the short/theme/book or series after the mainline listings.

Diecast characters are shown in their first year/motif release and then not shown again unless there was a major/significant design (variant) re-release. Through CARS 1, there were only a small handful of variants. For CARS 2, virtually every major character was released with a segmented plastic face and then replaced with a UNIBODY metal diecast body - sometimes just months later, for this checklist, in situations such as that, the only photo shown is the UNIBODY version as it's the "better" and more correct release form. For characters that were upgraded years later, then both are usually shown as they were released and later upgraded. Minor variants are ignored except you'll notice an extra check circle underneath. For CARS 3, most of the variants are major so both are shown.

The (Motor) Speedway South of 36 racers are NOT shown separately as if you have the set, clearly you have the entire set of Piston Cup racers - it seems more useful to list the Piston Cup racers as separate releases & year by year availability for collectors who did not want to open the MSOS itself and/or, for those who do not have the set and want to build as complete of a set as possible.

The final count and breakdown are on page 59.

Boost ○○

Chick Hicks ○

Dirt Track Lightning McQueen ○

DJ ○
(incorrect stripe)

Doc Hudson ○

Filmore/Fillmore ○

Flo ○

Guido ○

King/The King ○

Lightning McQueen ○
(no Rust-Eze spoiler decal)

Lizzie ○○○○

Guido ○

Mack ○
(plastic)

Mater ○

Ramone - Purple ○

Red ○

Rollin Bowlin Mater ○

Sally ○○

Sarge ○

Sheriff ○

Snot Rod ○

Stanley ○
(statue)

Tractor ○

Wingo ○

CARS are not necessarily in size or scale to each other. They are re-sized for grid conformity.
Double check circles indicate minor variant release that year. SEGMENTED or UNIBODY indicates first release of that production variant.

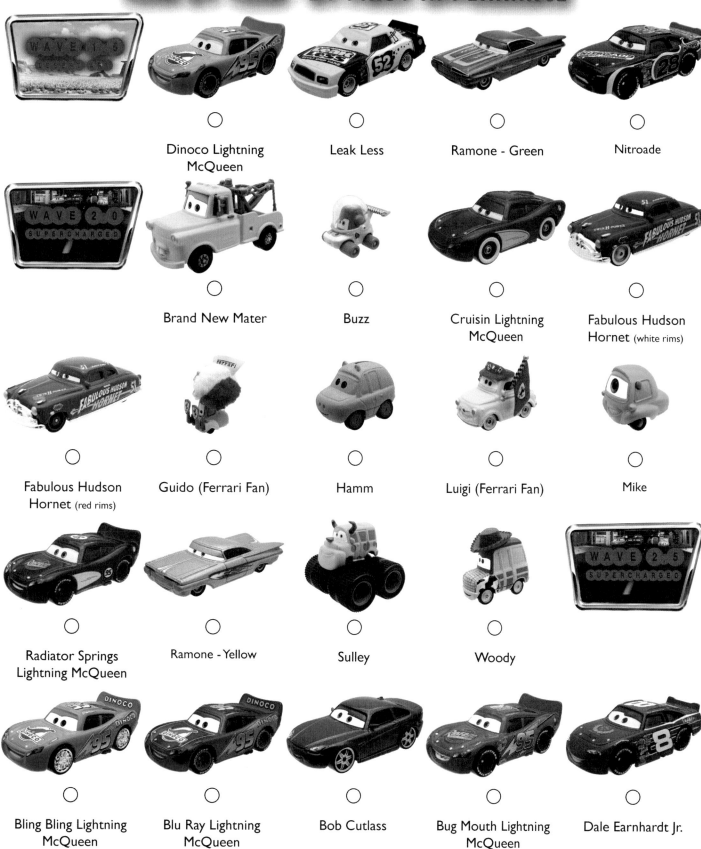

WAVE 1.5

○ Dinoco Lightning McQueen

○ Leak Less

○ Ramone - Green

○ Nitroade

WAVE 2.0 SUPERCHARGED

○ Brand New Mater

○ Buzz

○ Cruisin Lightning McQueen

○ Fabulous Hudson Hornet (white rims)

○ Fabulous Hudson Hornet (red rims)

○ Guido (Ferrari Fan)

○ Hamm

○ Luigi (Ferrari Fan)

○ Mike

○ Radiator Springs Lightning McQueen

○ Ramone - Yellow

○ Sulley

○ Woody

WAVE 2.5 SUPERCHARGED

○ Bling Bling Lightning McQueen

○ Blu Ray Lightning McQueen

○ Bob Cutlass

○ Bug Mouth Lightning McQueen

○ Dale Earnhardt Jr.

CARS are not necessarily in size or scale to each other. They are re-sized for grid conformity.
Double check circles indicate minor variant release that year. SEGMENTED or UNIBODY indicates first release of that production variant.

3

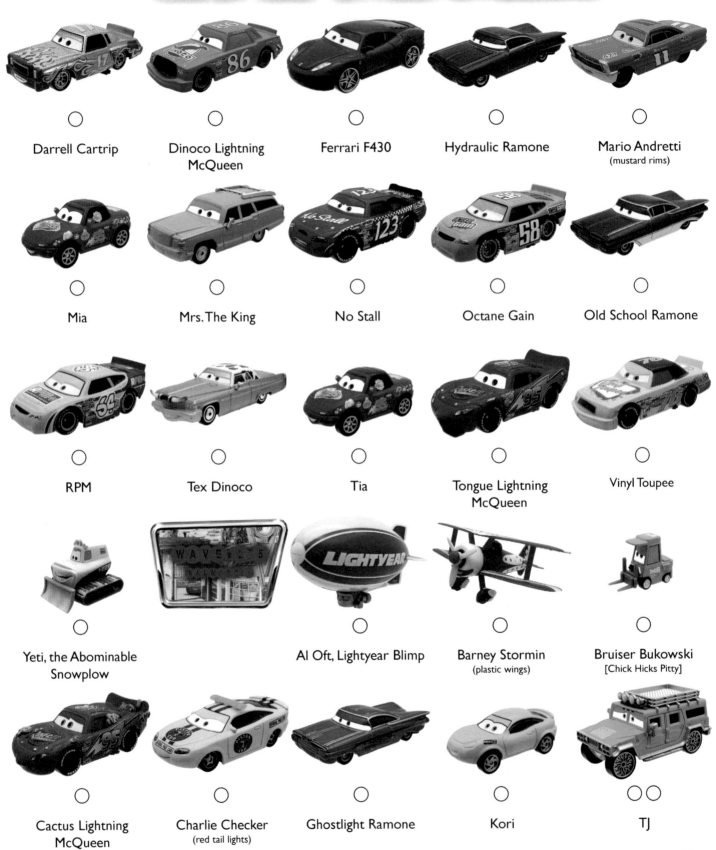

○	○	○	○	○
Darrell Cartrip	Dinoco Lightning McQueen	Ferrari F430	Hydraulic Ramone	Mario Andretti (mustard rims)
○	○	○	○	○
Mia	Mrs. The King	No Stall	Octane Gain	Old School Ramone
○	○	○	○	○
RPM	Tex Dinoco	Tia	Tongue Lightning McQueen	Vinyl Toupee
○		○	○	○
Yeti, the Abominable Snowplow		Al Oft, Lightyear Blimp	Barney Stormin (plastic wings)	Bruiser Bukowski [Chick Hicks Pitty]
○	○	○	○	○○
Cactus Lightning McQueen	Charlie Checker (red tail lights)	Ghostlight Ramone	Kori	TJ

CARS are not necessarily in size or scale to each other. They are re-sized for grid conformity.
Double check circles indicate minor variant release that year. SEGMENTED or UNIBODY indicates first release of that production variant.

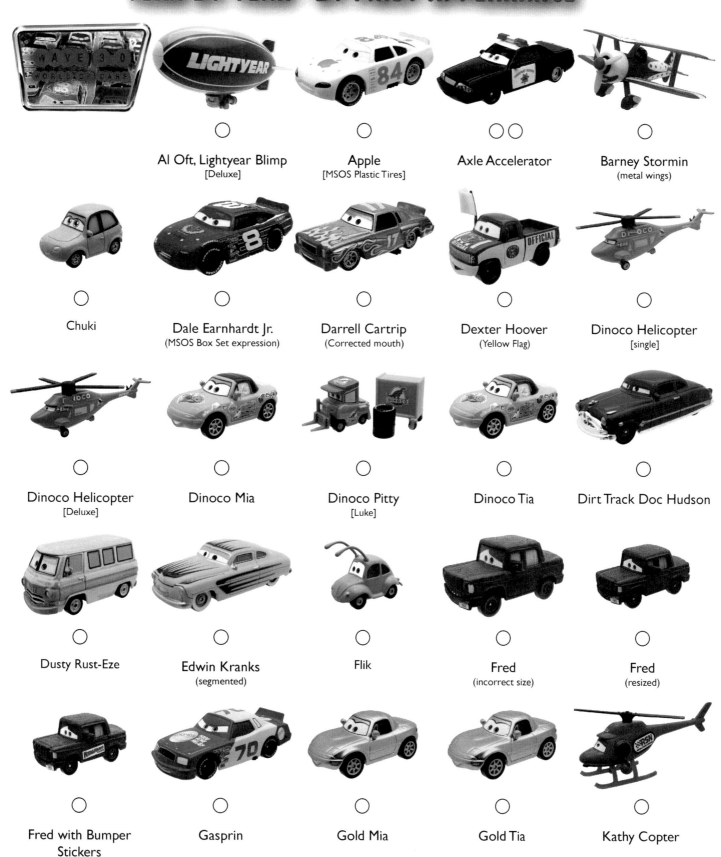

Al Oft, Lightyear Blimp
[Deluxe]

Apple
[MSOS Plastic Tires]

Axle Accelerator

Barney Stormin
(metal wings)

Chuki

Dale Earnhardt Jr.
(MSOS Box Set expression)

Darrell Cartrip
(Corrected mouth)

Dexter Hoover
(Yellow Flag)

Dinoco Helicopter
[single]

Dinoco Helicopter
[Deluxe]

Dinoco Mia

Dinoco Pitty
[Luke]

Dinoco Tia

Dirt Track Doc Hudson

Dusty Rust-Eze

Edwin Kranks
(segmented)

Flik

Fred
(incorrect size)

Fred
(resized)

Fred with Bumper
Stickers

Gasprin

Gold Mia

Gold Tia

Kathy Copter

CARS are not necessarily in size or scale to each other. They are re-sized for grid conformity.
Double check circles indicate minor variant release that year. SEGMENTED or UNIBODY indicates first release of that production variant.

5

○	○	○	○	○
Leak Less Crew Chief	Leak Less Pitty [Stacy]	Leroy Traffik	Lightning McQueen (segmented)	Lightning McQueen with Stickers
○	○	○	○	○
Lightning Ramone	Lightning Storm McQueen [SDCC]	Lightning Storm McQueen (segmented)	Marco	My Name is Not Chuck
○○	○	○	○	○
N20 Cola	No Stall Crew Chief	No Stall Pitty	Octane Gain Pitty	Pit Crew Member Fabulous HH
○	○	○	○	○
Pit Crew Member Fillmore	Pit Crew Member Guido	PT Flea	Race Official Tom	RPM Pitty [Petrol] (segmented)
○	○	○	○	○
Re-Volting	Rusty Rust-Eze	Sally with Cone (segmented)	Shiny Wax	Shiny Wax Crew Chief

CARS are not necessarily in size or scale to each other. They are re-sized for grid conformity.
Double check circles indicate minor variant release that year. SEGMENTED or UNIBODY indicates first release of that production variant.

6

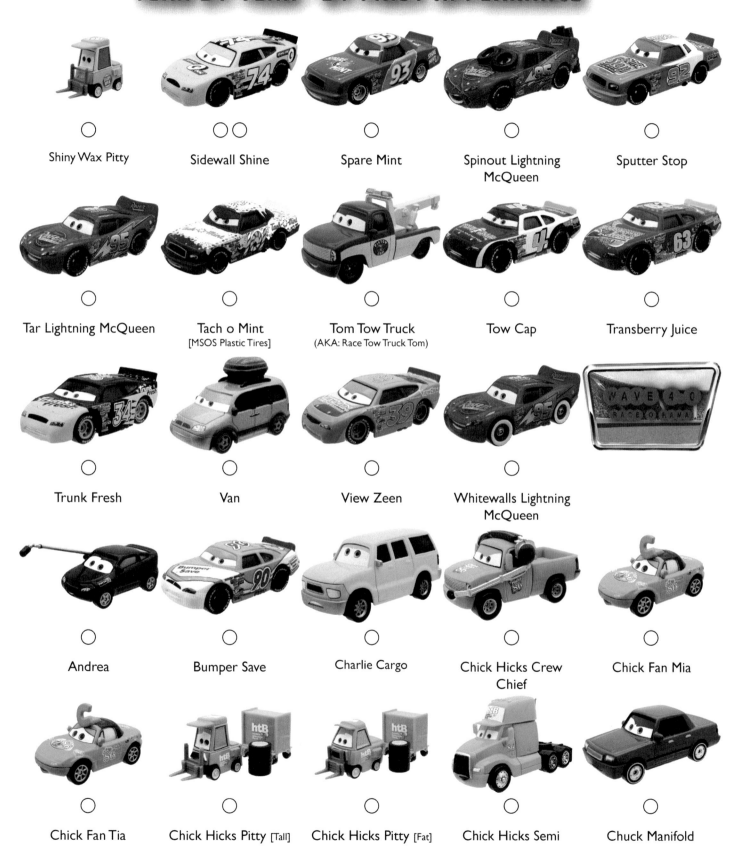

○	○ ○	○	○	○
Shiny Wax Pitty	Sidewall Shine	Spare Mint	Spinout Lightning McQueen	Sputter Stop
○	○	○	○	○
Tar Lightning McQueen	Tach o Mint [MSOS Plastic Tires]	Tom Tow Truck (AKA: Race Tow Truck Tom)	Tow Cap	Transberry Juice
○	○	○	○	
Trunk Fresh	Van	View Zeen	Whitewalls Lightning McQueen	
○	○	○	○	○
Andrea	Bumper Save	Charlie Cargo	Chick Hicks Crew Chief	Chick Fan Mia
○	○	○	○	○
Chick Fan Tia	Chick Hicks Pitty [Tall]	Chick Hicks Pitty [Fat]	Chick Hicks Semi	Chuck Manifold

CARS are not necessarily in size or scale to each other. They are re-sized for grid conformity.
Double check circles indicate minor variant release that year. SEGMENTED or UNIBODY indicates first release of that production variant.

7

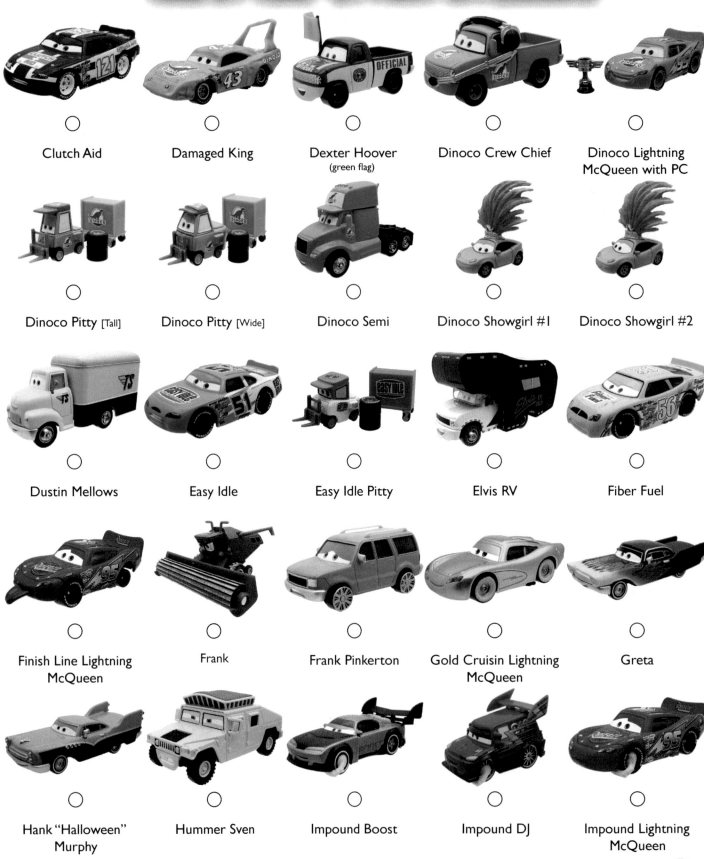

○	○	○	○	○
Clutch Aid	Damaged King	Dexter Hoover (green flag)	Dinoco Crew Chief	Dinoco Lightning McQueen with PC
○	○	○	○	○
Dinoco Pitty [Tall]	Dinoco Pitty [Wide]	Dinoco Semi	Dinoco Showgirl #1	Dinoco Showgirl #2
○	○	○	○	○
Dustin Mellows	Easy Idle	Easy Idle Pitty	Elvis RV	Fiber Fuel
○	○	○	○	○
Finish Line Lightning McQueen	Frank	Frank Pinkerton	Gold Cruisin Lightning McQueen	Greta
○	○	○	○	○
Hank "Halloween" Murphy	Hummer Sven	Impound Boost	Impound DJ	Impound Lightning McQueen

CARS are not necessarily in size or scale to each other. They are re-sized for grid conformity.
Double check circles indicate minor variant release that year. SEGMENTED or UNIBODY indicates first release of that production variant.

Take5aDay.com

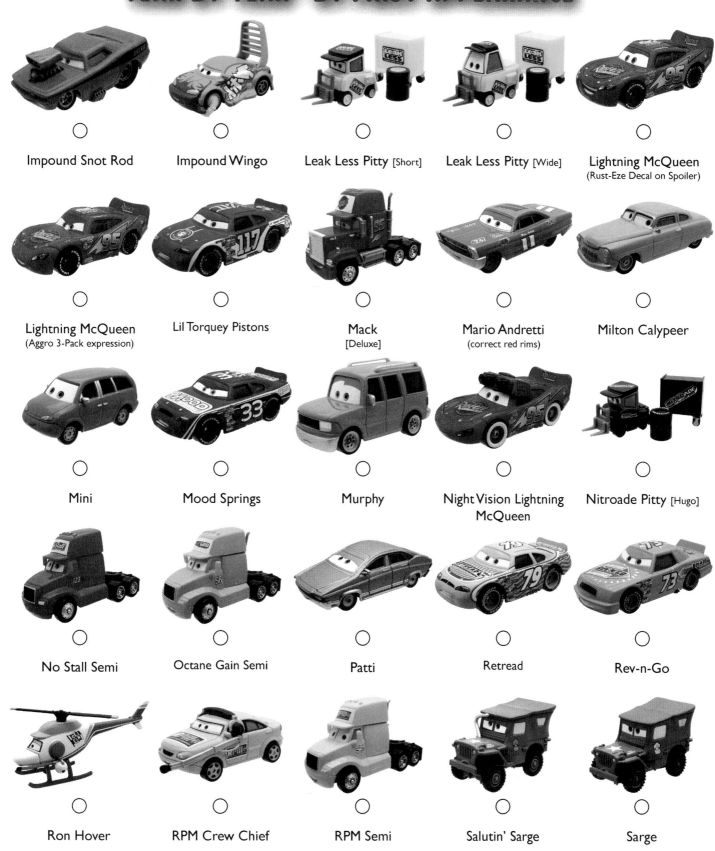

Impound Snot Rod

Impound Wingo

Leak Less Pitty [Short]

Leak Less Pitty [Wide]

Lightning McQueen (Rust-Eze Decal on Spoiler)

Lightning McQueen (Aggro 3-Pack expression)

Lil Torquey Pistons

Mack [Deluxe]

Mario Andretti (correct red rims)

Milton Calypeer

Mini

Mood Springs

Murphy

Night Vision Lightning McQueen

Nitroade Pitty [Hugo]

No Stall Semi

Octane Gain Semi

Patti

Retread

Rev-n-Go

Ron Hover

RPM Crew Chief

RPM Semi

Salutin' Sarge

Sarge

CARS are not necessarily in size or scale to each other. They are re-sized for grid conformity.
Double check circles indicate minor variant release that year. SEGMENTED or UNIBODY indicates first release of that production variant.

9

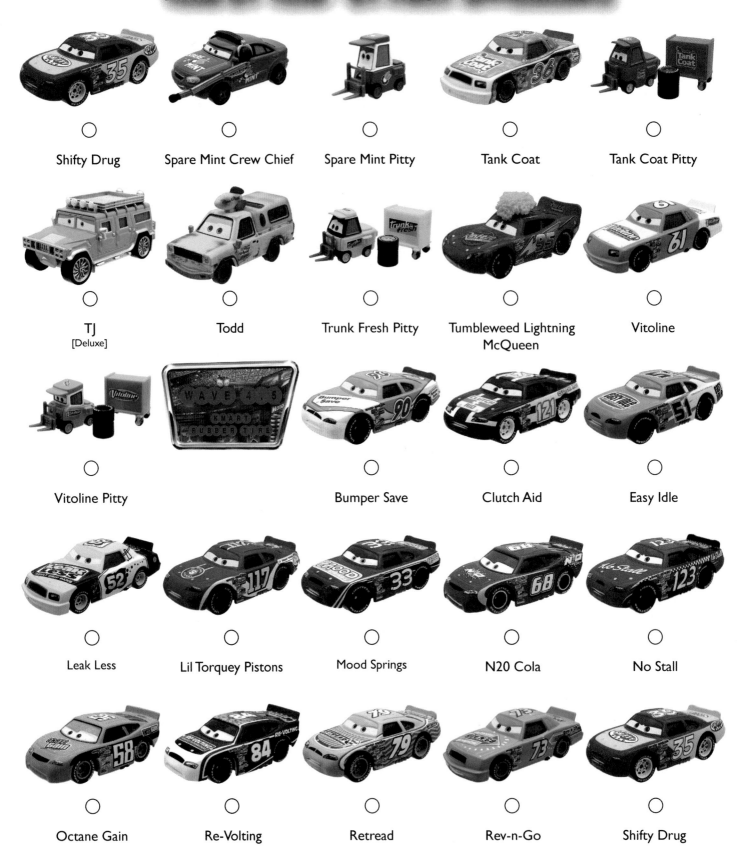

○	○	○	○	○
Shifty Drug	Spare Mint Crew Chief	Spare Mint Pitty	Tank Coat	Tank Coat Pitty
○	○	○	○	○
TJ [Deluxe]	Todd	Trunk Fresh Pitty	Tumbleweed Lightning McQueen	Vitoline
○	○	○	○	○
Vitoline Pitty		Bumper Save	Clutch Aid	Easy Idle
○	○	○	○	○
Leak Less	Lil Torquey Pistons	Mood Springs	N20 Cola	No Stall
○	○	○	○	○
Octane Gain	Re-Volting	Retread	Rev-n-Go	Shifty Drug

CARS are not necessarily in size or scale to each other. They are re-sized for grid conformity.
Double check circles indicate minor variant release that year. SEGMENTED or UNIBODY indicates first release of that production variant.

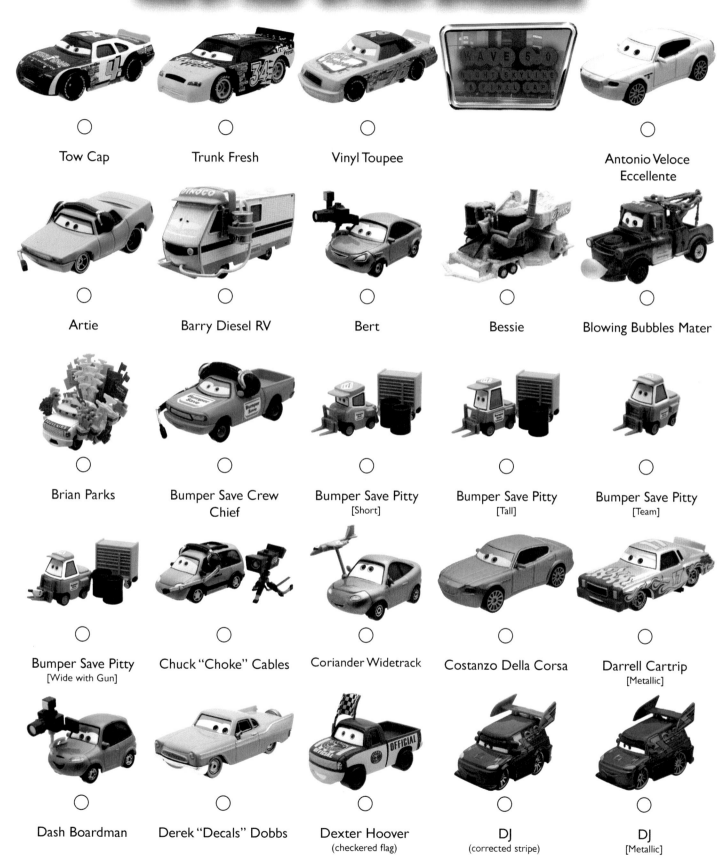

Tow Cap

Trunk Fresh

Vinyl Toupee

Antonio Veloce Eccellente

Artie

Barry Diesel RV

Bert

Bessie

Blowing Bubbles Mater

Brian Parks

Bumper Save Crew Chief

Bumper Save Pitty
[Short]

Bumper Save Pitty
[Tall]

Bumper Save Pitty
[Team]

Bumper Save Pitty
[Wide with Gun]

Chuck "Choke" Cables

Coriander Widetrack

Costanzo Della Corsa

Darrell Cartrip
[Metallic]

Dash Boardman

Derek "Decals" Dobbs

Dexter Hoover
(checkered flag)

DJ
(corrected stripe)

DJ
[Metallic]

CARS are not necessarily in size or scale to each other. They are re-sized for grid conformity.
Double check circles indicate minor variant release that year. SEGMENTED or UNIBODY indicates first release of that production variant.

11

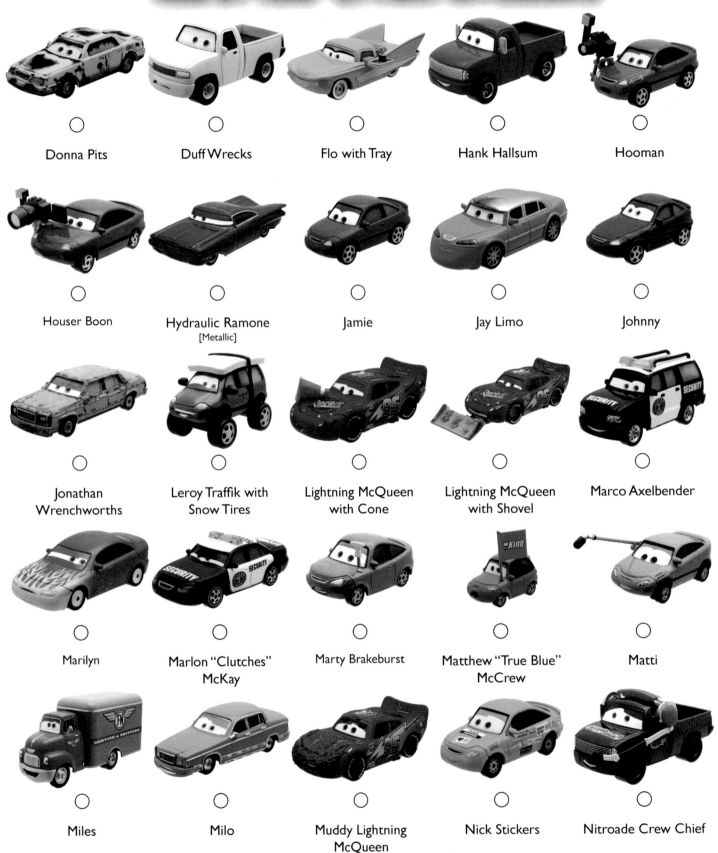

Donna Pits

Duff Wrecks

Flo with Tray

Hank Hallsum

Hooman

Houser Boon

Hydraulic Ramone
[Metallic]

Jamie

Jay Limo

Johnny

Jonathan
Wrenchworths

Leroy Traffik with
Snow Tires

Lightning McQueen
with Cone

Lightning McQueen
with Shovel

Marco Axelbender

Marilyn

Marlon "Clutches"
McKay

Marty Brakeburst

Matthew "True Blue"
McCrew

Matti

Miles

Milo

Muddy Lightning
McQueen

Nick Stickers

Nitroade Crew Chief

CARS are not necessarily in size or scale to each other. They are re-sized for grid conformity.
Double check circles indicate minor variant release that year. SEGMENTED or UNIBODY indicates first release of that production variant.

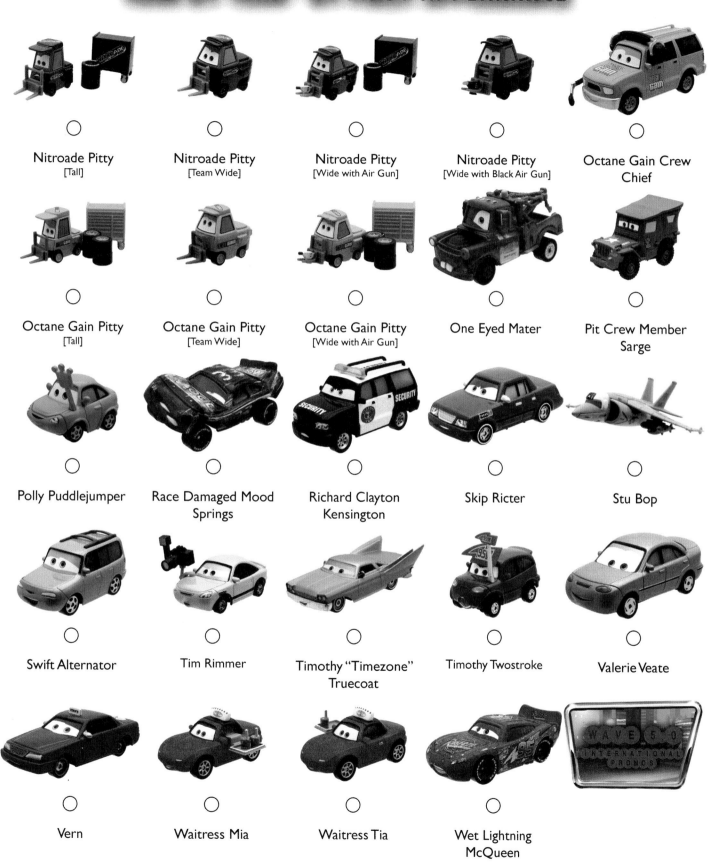

Nitroade Pitty [Tall]

Nitroade Pitty [Team Wide]

Nitroade Pitty [Wide with Air Gun]

Nitroade Pitty [Wide with Black Air Gun]

Octane Gain Crew Chief

Octane Gain Pitty [Tall]

Octane Gain Pitty [Team Wide]

Octane Gain Pitty [Wide with Air Gun]

One Eyed Mater

Pit Crew Member Sarge

Polly Puddlejumper

Race Damaged Mood Springs

Richard Clayton Kensington

Skip Ricter

Stu Bop

Swift Alternator

Tim Rimmer

Timothy "Timezone" Truecoat

Timothy Twostroke

Valerie Veate

Vern

Waitress Mia

Waitress Tia

Wet Lightning McQueen

CARS are not necessarily in size or scale to each other. They are re-sized for grid conformity.
Double check circles indicate minor variant release that year. SEGMENTED or UNIBODY indicates first release of that production variant.

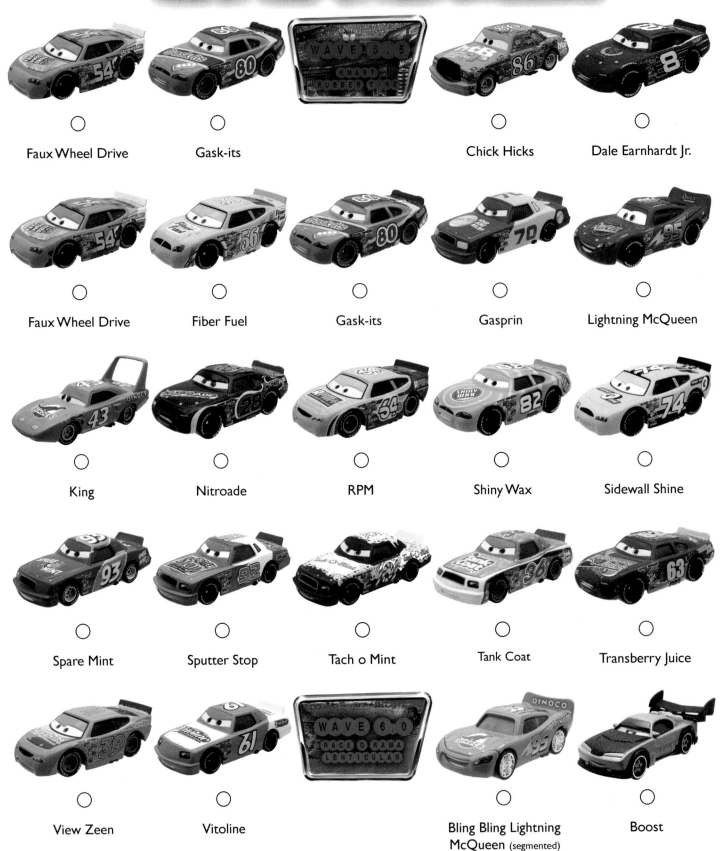

Faux Wheel Drive   Gask-its   Chick Hicks   Dale Earnhardt Jr.

Faux Wheel Drive   Fiber Fuel   Gask-its   Gasprin   Lightning McQueen

King   Nitroade   RPM   Shiny Wax   Sidewall Shine

Spare Mint   Sputter Stop   Tach o Mint   Tank Coat   Transberry Juice

View Zeen   Vitoline   Bling Bling Lightning   Boost
                                                                McQueen (segmented)

14

CARS are not necessarily in size or scale to each other. They are re-sized for grid conformity.
Double check circles indicate minor variant release that year. SEGMENTED or UNIBODY indicates first release of that production variant.

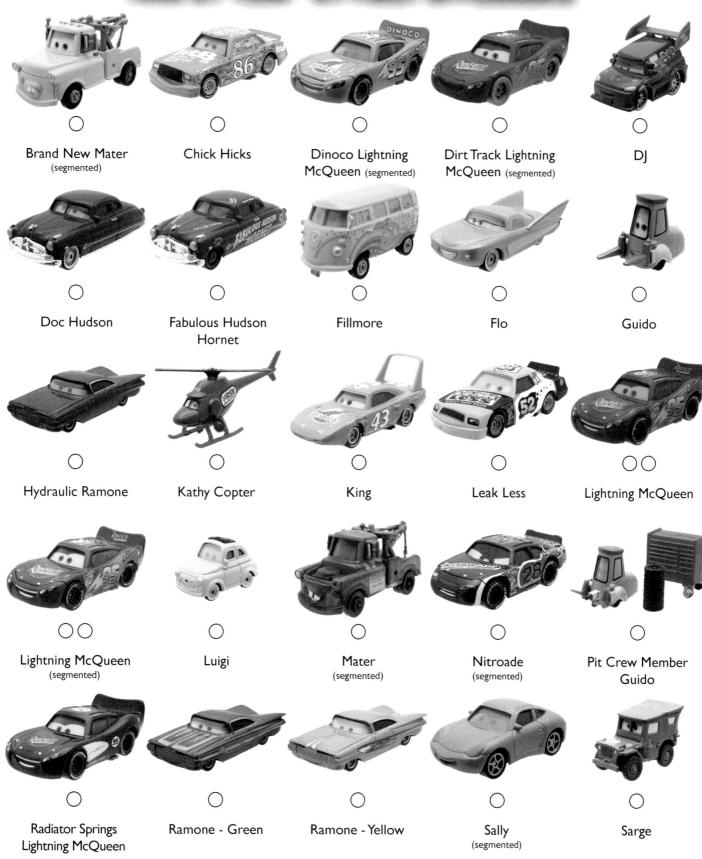

○ Brand New Mater (segmented)

○ Chick Hicks

○ Dinoco Lightning McQueen (segmented)

○ Dirt Track Lightning McQueen (segmented)

○ DJ

○ Doc Hudson

○ Fabulous Hudson Hornet

○ Fillmore

○ Flo

○ Guido

○ Hydraulic Ramone

○ Kathy Copter

○ King

○ Leak Less

○○ Lightning McQueen

○○ Lightning McQueen (segmented)

○ Luigi

○ Mater (segmented)

○ Nitroade (segmented)

○ Pit Crew Member Guido

○ Radiator Springs Lightning McQueen

○ Ramone - Green

○ Ramone - Yellow

○ Sally (segmented)

○ Sarge

CARS are not necessarily in size or scale to each other. They are re-sized for grid conformity.
Double check circles indicate minor variant release that year. SEGMENTED or UNIBODY indicates first release of that production variant.

15

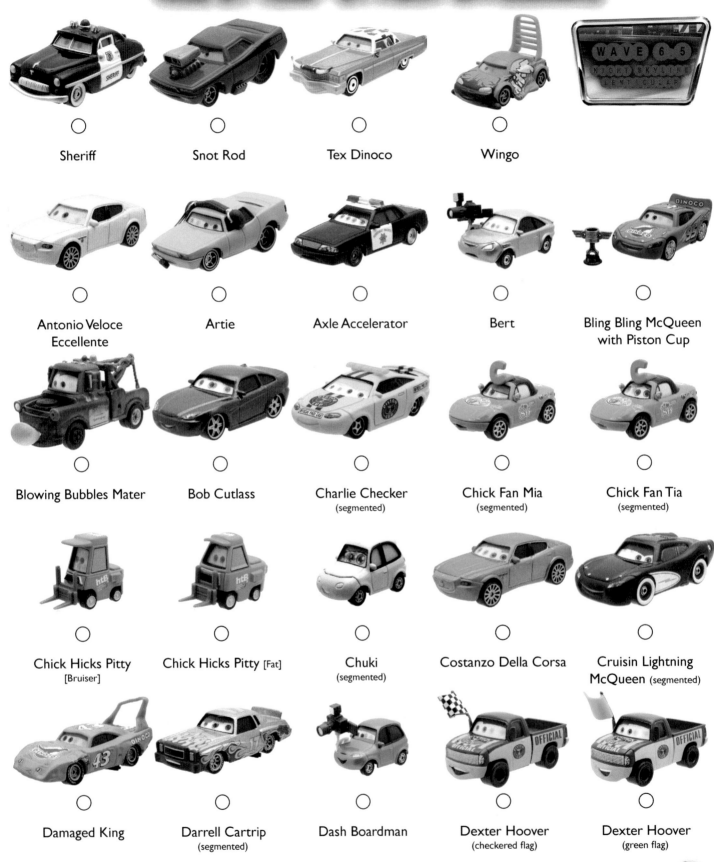

Sheriff

Snot Rod

Tex Dinoco

Wingo

WAVE 6 5
NIGHT SKYLINE
LENTICULAR

Antonio Veloce Eccellente

Artie

Axle Accelerator

Bert

Bling Bling McQueen with Piston Cup

Blowing Bubbles Mater

Bob Cutlass

Charlie Checker
(segmented)

Chick Fan Mia
(segmented)

Chick Fan Tia
(segmented)

Chick Hicks Pitty
[Bruiser]

Chick Hicks Pitty [Fat]

Chuki
(segmented)

Costanzo Della Corsa

Cruisin Lightning McQueen (segmented)

Damaged King

Darrell Cartrip
(segmented)

Dash Boardman

Dexter Hoover
(checkered flag)

Dexter Hoover
(green flag)

CARS are not necessarily in size or scale to each other. They are re-sized for grid conformity.
Double check circles indicate minor variant release that year. SEGMENTED or UNIBODY indicates first release of that production variant.

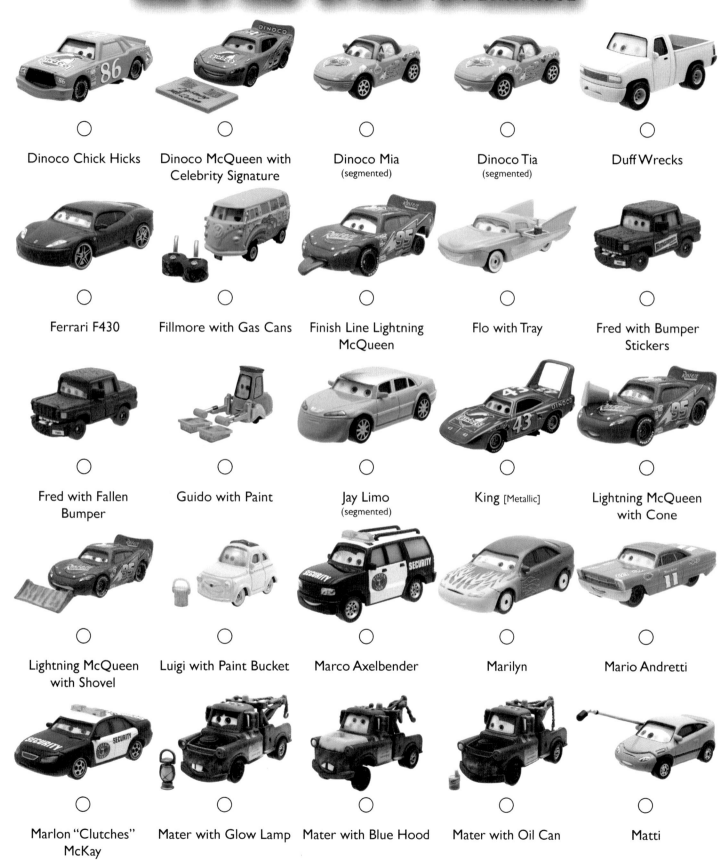

Dinoco Chick Hicks

Dinoco McQueen with Celebrity Signature

Dinoco Mia (segmented)

Dinoco Tia (segmented)

Duff Wrecks

Ferrari F430

Fillmore with Gas Cans

Finish Line Lightning McQueen

Flo with Tray

Fred with Bumper Stickers

Fred with Fallen Bumper

Guido with Paint

Jay Limo (segmented)

King [Metallic]

Lightning McQueen with Cone

Lightning McQueen with Shovel

Luigi with Paint Bucket

Marco Axelbender

Marilyn

Mario Andretti

Marlon "Clutches" McKay

Mater with Glow Lamp

Mater with Blue Hood

Mater with Oil Can

Matti

CARS are not necessarily in size or scale to each other. They are re-sized for grid conformity.
Double check circles indicate minor variant release that year. SEGMENTED or UNIBODY indicates first release of that production variant.

17

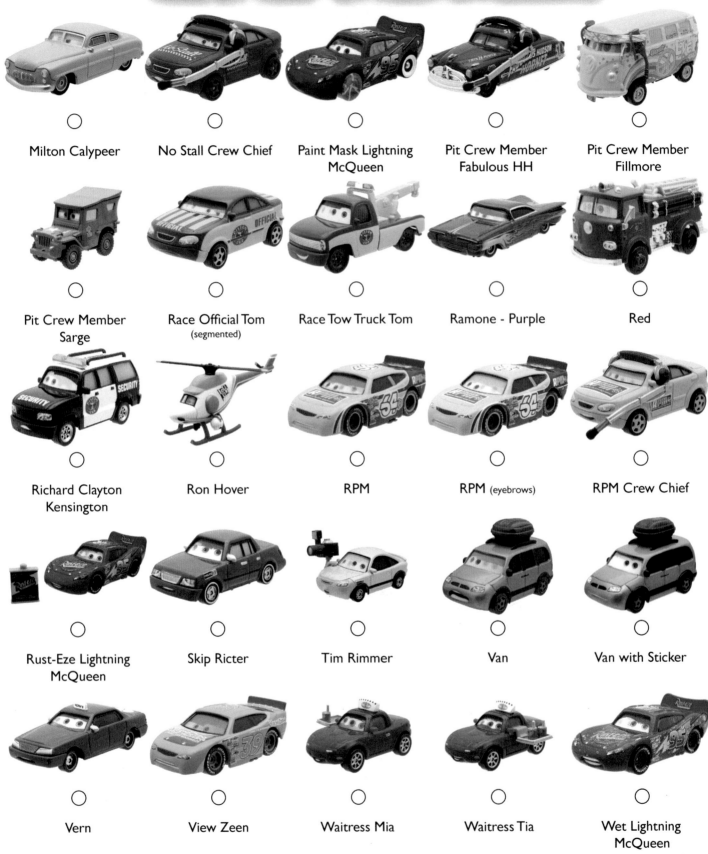

Milton Calypeer	No Stall Crew Chief	Paint Mask Lightning McQueen	Pit Crew Member Fabulous HH	Pit Crew Member Fillmore
Pit Crew Member Sarge	Race Official Tom (segmented)	Race Tow Truck Tom	Ramone - Purple	Red
Richard Clayton Kensington	Ron Hover	RPM	RPM (eyebrows)	RPM Crew Chief
Rust-Eze Lightning McQueen	Skip Ricter	Tim Rimmer	Van	Van with Sticker
Vern	View Zeen	Waitress Mia	Waitress Tia	Wet Lightning McQueen

CARS are not necessarily in size or scale to each other. They are re-sized for grid conformity.
Double check circles indicate minor variant release that year. SEGMENTED or UNIBODY indicates first release of that production variant.

Take5aDay.com

Whitewalls Lightning McQueen

Wilmar Flatz

Yeti, the Abominable Snowplow

Yeti with Snow Cones

Acer

Acer with Helmet

Acer with Torch

Alex Vandel

Alexander Hugo with Party Hat

Becky Wheelin

Bindo

Brent Mustangberger

Bruno Motoreau

Carla Veloso

Carlo Maserati

Cartney Brakin

Celine Dephare

Cruz Besouro

Damaged Rod Torque Redline

Darrell Cartrip

David Hobbscapp

Denise Beam

Don Crumlin

Double Decker Bus

CARS are not necessarily in size or scale to each other. They are re-sized for grid conformity.
Double check circles indicate minor variant release that year. SEGMENTED or UNIBODY indicates first release of that production variant.

19

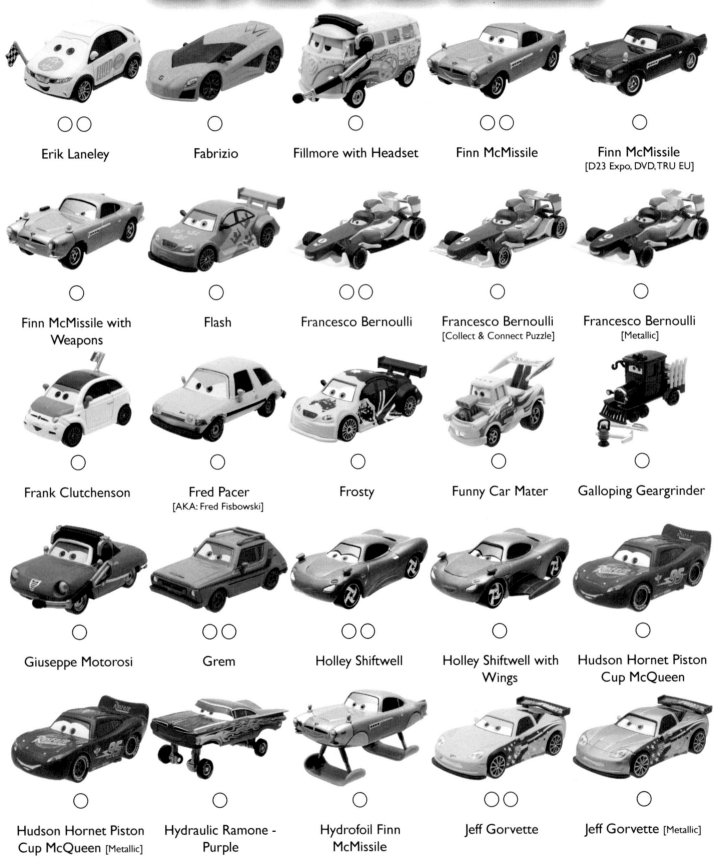

Erik Laneley

Fabrizio

Fillmore with Headset

Finn McMissile

Finn McMissile
[D23 Expo, DVD, TRU EU]

Finn McMissile with
Weapons

Flash

Francesco Bernoulli

Francesco Bernoulli
[Collect & Connect Puzzle]

Francesco Bernoulli
[Metallic]

Frank Clutchenson

Fred Pacer
[AKA: Fred Fisbowski]

Frosty

Funny Car Mater

Galloping Geargrinder

Giuseppe Motorosi

Grem

Holley Shiftwell

Holley Shiftwell with
Wings

Hudson Hornet Piston
Cup McQueen

Hudson Hornet Piston
Cup McQueen [Metallic]

Hydraulic Ramone -
Purple

Hydrofoil Finn
McMissile

Jeff Gorvette

Jeff Gorvette [Metallic]

CARS are not necessarily in size or scale to each other. They are re-sized for grid conformity.
Double check circles indicate minor variant release that year. SEGMENTED or UNIBODY indicates first release of that production variant.

Take5aDay.com

John Lassetire ○

Ka-Ciao Lightning McQueen ○

Kabuto (UNIBODY) ○

Kimura Kaizo ○

Kingpin Nobunaga ○

Leland Turbo ○

Lewis Hamilton ○○

Lightning McQueen with Party Wheels ○

Lightning McQueen Racing Wheels ○

Lightning McQueen Racing Wheels ○○

Lightning McQueen Racing Wheels (box set) ○

Lightning McQueen Racing Wheels (launcher) ○

Lightning McQueen [Metallic] ○

Lightning McQueen [Collect & Connect Puzzle] ○

Lightning McQueen [Finish Line Frenzy - Gold] ○

Lightning McQueen [Finish Line Frenzy - Silver] ○

Lightning McQueen with Travel Wheels ○

Long Ge ○

Mama Bernoulli ○

Mama Topolino (segmented) ○

Mary Esgocar ○

Mater [Collect & Connect Puzzle] ○

Mater with Spy Glasses ○

Max Schnell ○○

Mel Dorado ○

CARS are not necessarily in size or scale to each other. They are re-sized for grid conformity.
Double check circles indicate minor variant release that year. SEGMENTED or UNIBODY indicates first release of that production variant.

21

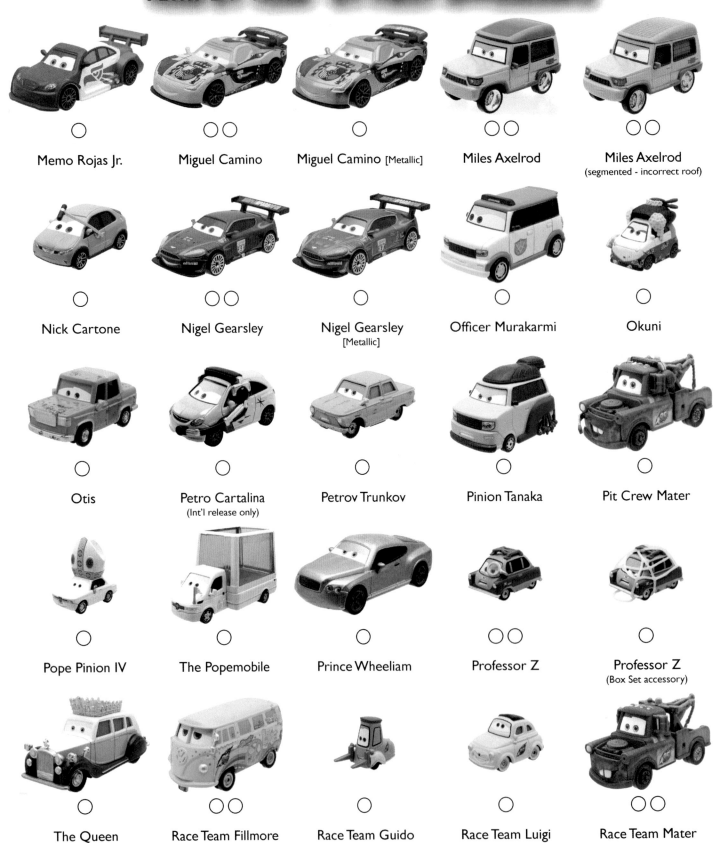

Memo Rojas Jr.

Miguel Camino

Miguel Camino [Metallic]

Miles Axelrod

Miles Axelrod
(segmented - incorrect roof)

Nick Cartone

Nigel Gearsley

Nigel Gearsley
[Metallic]

Officer Murakarmi

Okuni

Otis

Petro Cartalina
(Int'l release only)

Petrov Trunkov

Pinion Tanaka

Pit Crew Mater

Pope Pinion IV

The Popemobile

Prince Wheeliam

Professor Z

Professor Z
(Box Set accessory)

The Queen

Race Team Fillmore

Race Team Guido

Race Team Luigi

Race Team Mater

CARS are not necessarily in size or scale to each other. They are re-sized for grid conformity.
Double check circles indicate minor variant release that year. SEGMENTED or UNIBODY indicates first release of that production variant.

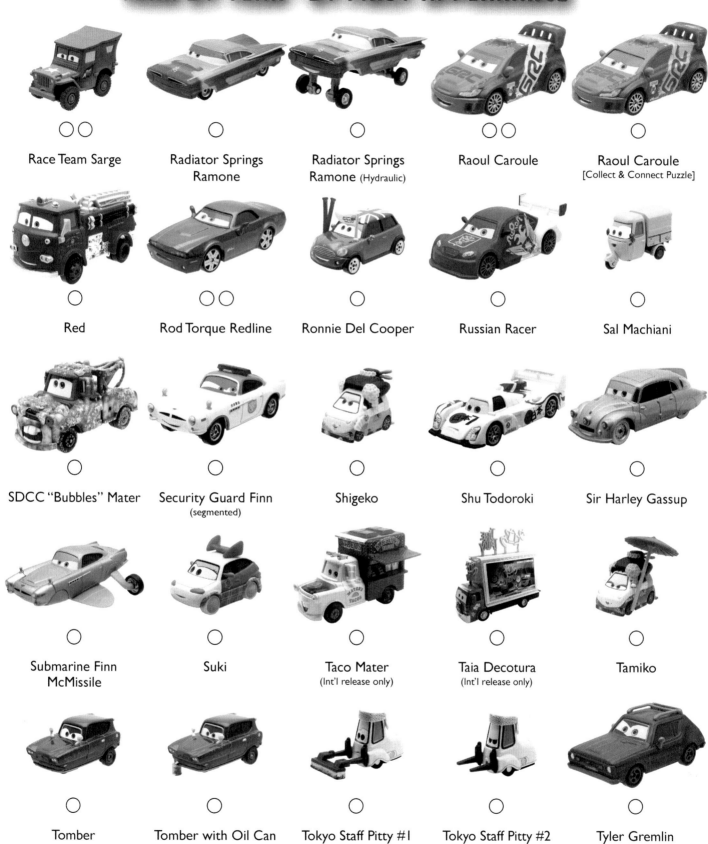

Race Team Sarge

Radiator Springs Ramone

Radiator Springs Ramone (Hydraulic)

Raoul Caroule

Raoul Caroule [Collect & Connect Puzzle]

Red

Rod Torque Redline

Ronnie Del Cooper

Russian Racer

Sal Machiani

SDCC "Bubbles" Mater

Security Guard Finn (segmented)

Shigeko

Shu Todoroki

Sir Harley Gassup

Submarine Finn McMissile

Suki

Taco Mater (Int'l release only)

Taia Decotura (Int'l release only)

Tamiko

Tomber

Tomber with Oil Can

Tokyo Staff Pitty #1

Tokyo Staff Pitty #2

Tyler Gremlin

CARS are not necessarily in size or scale to each other. They are re-sized for grid conformity.
Double check circles indicate minor variant release that year. SEGMENTED or UNIBODY indicates first release of that production variant.

Uncle Topolino

Uncle Topolino with Tires

Union Jack Ramone

Victor H.

Vladimir Trunkov

Wasabi Mater

You Da Bomb Mater

You the Bomb Mater

Zen Pitty

Carla Veloso

Francesco Bernoulli

Jeff Gorvette
(with logo - Int'l only)

Lewis Hamilton

Lightning McQueen with Racing Wheel

Max Schnell

Miguel Camino

Nigel Gearsley

Roule Caroule

Shu Todoroki

Airport Mater

Alex Carvill

Alloy Hemberger

Austin Littleton

24

CARS are not necessarily in size or scale to each other. They are re-sized for grid conformity.
Double check circles indicate minor variant release that year. SEGMENTED or UNIBODY indicates first release of that production variant.

Body Shop Ramone
(with paint spray gun)

Boost with Flames

Brent Mustangberger with Headset

Chauncy Fares

Chisaki

Clutch Foster

Convoy Brothers "G"

Convoy Brothers "I"

Convoy Brothers "K"

Convoy Brothers "N"

Darrell Cartrip with Headset

David Hobbscapp with Headset

DJ with Flames

Donna Pits
(UNIBODY)

Doug Speedcheck

Dracula Mater

Edwin Kranks
(UNIBODY)

Franca

Francesca

Franceco Fan Mater

Fred
(UNIBODY)

Frosty
[Metallic Silver - AUS Only]

Grem with Weapon

Guido with Glasses

Harumi

CARS are not necessarily in size or scale to each other. They are re-sized for grid conformity.
Double check circles indicate minor variant release that year. SEGMENTED or UNIBODY indicates first release of that production variant.

25

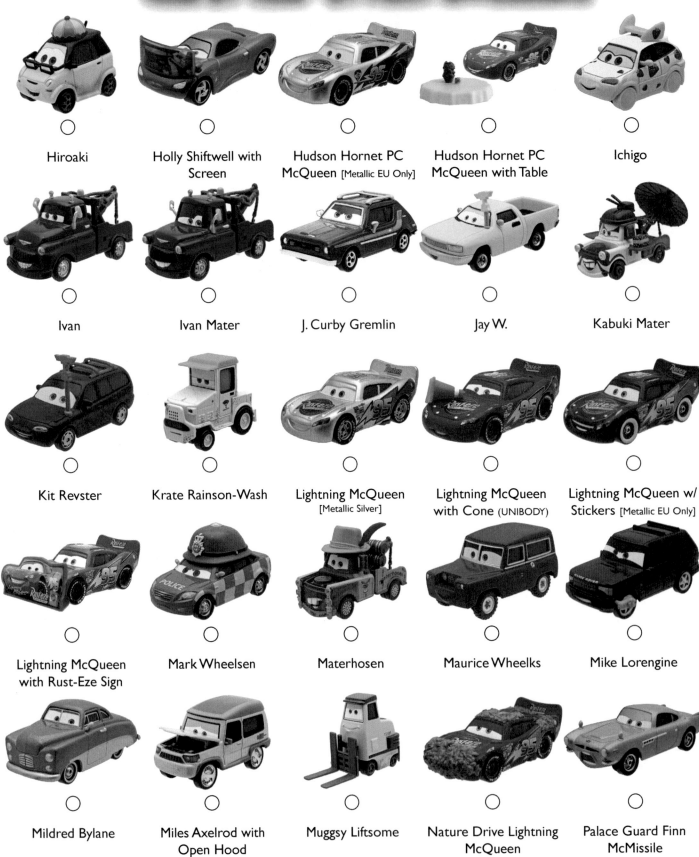

Hiroaki	Holly Shiftwell with Screen	Hudson Hornet PC McQueen [Metallic EU Only]	Hudson Hornet PC McQueen with Table	Ichigo
Ivan	Ivan Mater	J. Curby Gremlin	Jay W.	Kabuki Mater
Kit Revster	Krate Rainson-Wash	Lightning McQueen [Metallic Silver]	Lightning McQueen with Cone (UNIBODY)	Lightning McQueen w/ Stickers [Metallic EU Only]
Lightning McQueen with Rust-Eze Sign	Mark Wheelsen	Materhosen	Maurice Wheelks	Mike Lorengine
Mildred Bylane	Miles Axelrod with Open Hood	Muggsy Liftsome	Nature Drive Lightning McQueen	Palace Guard Finn McMissile

CARS are not necessarily in size or scale to each other. They are re-sized for grid conformity.
Double check circles indicate minor variant release that year. SEGMENTED or UNIBODY indicates first release of that production variant.

Take5aDay.com

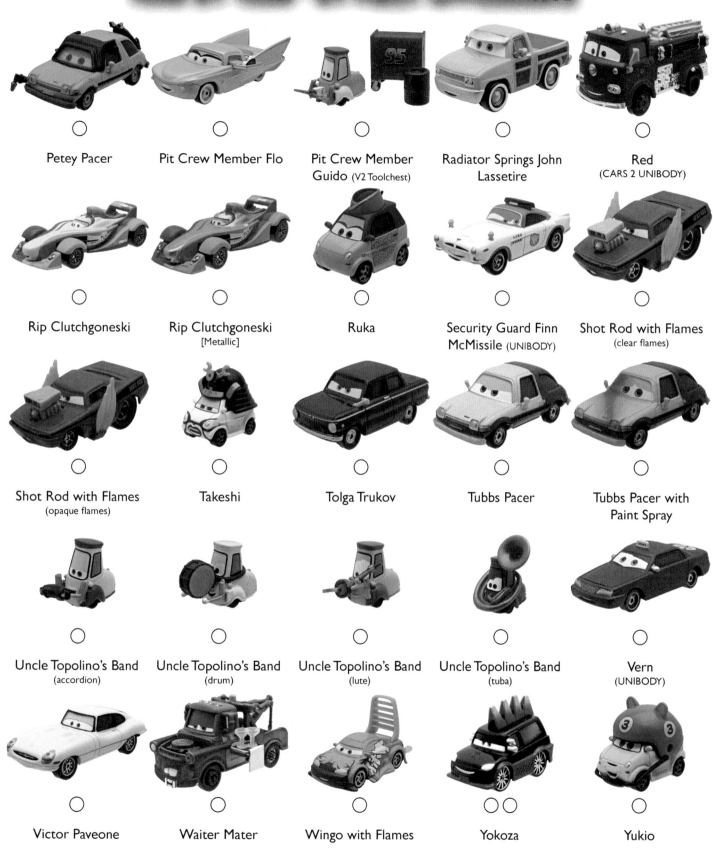

Petey Pacer

Pit Crew Member Flo

Pit Crew Member
Guido (V2 Toolchest)

Radiator Springs John
Lassetire

Red
(CARS 2 UNIBODY)

Rip Clutchgoneski

Rip Clutchgoneski
[Metallic]

Ruka

Security Guard Finn
McMissile (UNIBODY)

Shot Rod with Flames
(clear flames)

Shot Rod with Flames
(opaque flames)

Takeshi

Tolga Trukov

Tubbs Pacer

Tubbs Pacer with
Paint Spray

Uncle Topolino's Band
(accordion)

Uncle Topolino's Band
(drum)

Uncle Topolino's Band
(lute)

Uncle Topolino's Band
(tuba)

Vern
(UNIBODY)

Victor Paveone

Waiter Mater

Wingo with Flames

Yokoza

Yukio

CARS are not necessarily in size or scale to each other. They are re-sized for grid conformity.
Double check circles indicate minor variant release that year. SEGMENTED or UNIBODY indicates first release of that production variant.

27

	"95 Fan" Guido	"95 Fan" Luigi	Acer with Headset	Alberto
Alfredo	Carateka	Cardinal Antonio	Cardinal Angelo	Carinne Cavvy
Carla Veloso with Flames	Chuck "Choke" Cables (UNIBODY)	Ciao Francesco [With Allinol Bottle]	Cora Copper	Denise Beam (UNIBODY)
Geartrude	"Gee-Kuu" (TOMY RELEASE) [With Removable Headset]	Grem with Camera	Henri Motisse [With Paint Easel accessory]	Holley with Screen (VER 2 - DIFFERENT SCREEN)
Hydraulic Ramone (FLAT WINDSHIELD)	Interview Francesco	Jessica Giampetrol	John	Jonathan Shiftko

CARS are not necessarily in size or scale to each other. They are re-sized for grid conformity.
Double check circles indicate minor variant release that year. SEGMENTED or UNIBODY indicates first release of that production variant.

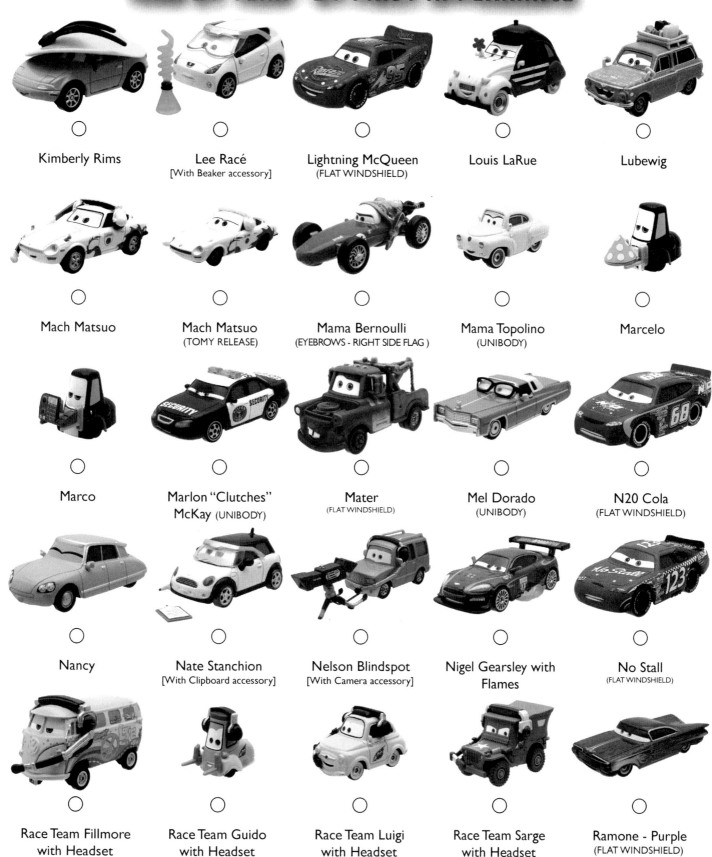

Kimberly Rims

Lee Racé
[With Beaker accessory]

Lightning McQueen
(FLAT WINDSHIELD)

Louis LaRue

Lubewig

Mach Matsuo

Mach Matsuo
(TOMY RELEASE)

Mama Bernoulli
(EYEBROWS - RIGHT SIDE FLAG)

Mama Topolino
(UNIBODY)

Marcelo

Marco

Marlon "Clutches"
McKay (UNIBODY)

Mater
(FLAT WINDSHIELD)

Mel Dorado
(UNIBODY)

N20 Cola
(FLAT WINDSHIELD)

Nancy

Nate Stanchion
[With Clipboard accessory]

Nelson Blindspot
[With Camera accessory]

Nigel Gearsley with
Flames

No Stall
(FLAT WINDSHIELD)

Race Team Fillmore
with Headset

Race Team Guido
with Headset

Race Team Luigi
with Headset

Race Team Sarge
with Headset

Ramone - Purple
(FLAT WINDSHIELD)

CARS are not necessarily in size or scale to each other. They are re-sized for grid conformity.
Double check circles indicate minor variant release that year. SEGMENTED or UNIBODY indicates first release of that production variant.

29

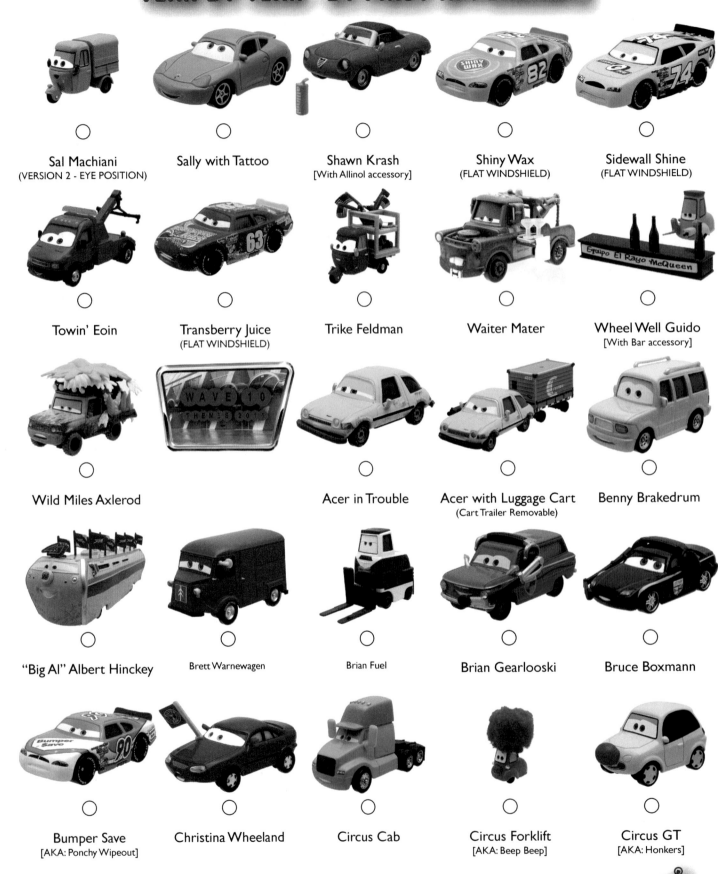

Sal Machiani
(VERSION 2 - EYE POSITION)

Sally with Tattoo

Shawn Krash
[With Allinol accessory]

Shiny Wax
(FLAT WINDSHIELD)

Sidewall Shine
(FLAT WINDSHIELD)

Towin' Eoin

Transberry Juice
(FLAT WINDSHIELD)

Trike Feldman

Waiter Mater

Wheel Well Guido
[With Bar accessory]

Wild Miles Axlerod

Acer in Trouble

Acer with Luggage Cart
(Cart Trailer Removable)

Benny Brakedrum

"Big Al" Albert Hinckey

Brett Warnewagen

Brian Fuel

Brian Gearlooski

Bruce Boxmann

Bumper Save
[AKA: Ponchy Wipeout]

Christina Wheeland

Circus Cab

Circus Forklift
[AKA: Beep Beep]

Circus GT
[AKA: Honkers]

CARS are not necessarily in size or scale to each other. They are re-sized for grid conformity.
Double check circles indicate minor variant release that year. SEGMENTED or UNIBODY indicates first release of that production variant.

Take5aDay.com

Circus Pickup
[AKA: Rimso]

Circus Sedan
[AKA: Clutchy]

Circus GT
[AKA: Blinkie]

Cruisin' Lightning McQueen (Flat Windshield)

Dashu Tsashimi

Determined Lightning McQueen

Dinoco Lightning McQueen (Flat Windshield)

Doug RM

Easy Idle
[AKA: Ruby "Easy" Oaks]

Easy Idle Pitty
(UNIBODY)

Edamame Tsashimi

Fabulous Hudson Hornet

Gearett Taylor

Grem in Trouble

Hydraulic Lightning Ramone

Jumpstart J. Ward

Kathy Copter
(UNIBODY)

Larry Camper

Lost in Desert Mini

Lost in Desert Van

M. Fenderickson

Manny Roadriquez

Mater (FLAT WINDSHIELD V2 - TRU Box Set)

Mater with Allinol Cans

Mater with Sign

CARS are not necessarily in size or scale to each other. They are re-sized for grid conformity.
Double check circles indicate minor variant release that year. SEGMENTED or UNIBODY indicates first release of that production variant.

31

○	○	○	○	○
Michael Honksel	Mike Fuse	Miles Axelrod with Microphone	My Name is Not Chuck with Cart	Nate McLugnut
○	○	○	○	○
Paul Oilkley	Pit Crew Member Mack	Pit Crew Member Sarge	Radiator Springs McQueen	Road Repair Lightning McQueen
○	○	○	○	○
RPM Pitty [AKA: Petrol Pulaski] (UNIBODY)	Sajan Karia	Sally (FLAT WINDSHIELD)	Scott Motorese	Scott Spark
○	○	○	○	○
Shifty Drug (Corrected PINK)	Shifty Drug [AKA: Kevin Racingtire]	Siren Carbarini	Superfan Mia	Superfan Tia
○	○	○	○	○
Tach O Mint	Tar Lightning McQueen (FLAT WINDSHIELD)	Terry Gong	Trent Crow-Tow (Trailer Removable)	Ucchi

CARS are not necessarily in size or scale to each other. They are re-sized for grid conformity.
Double check circles indicate minor variant release that year. SEGMENTED or UNIBODY indicates first release of that production variant.

Take5aDay.com

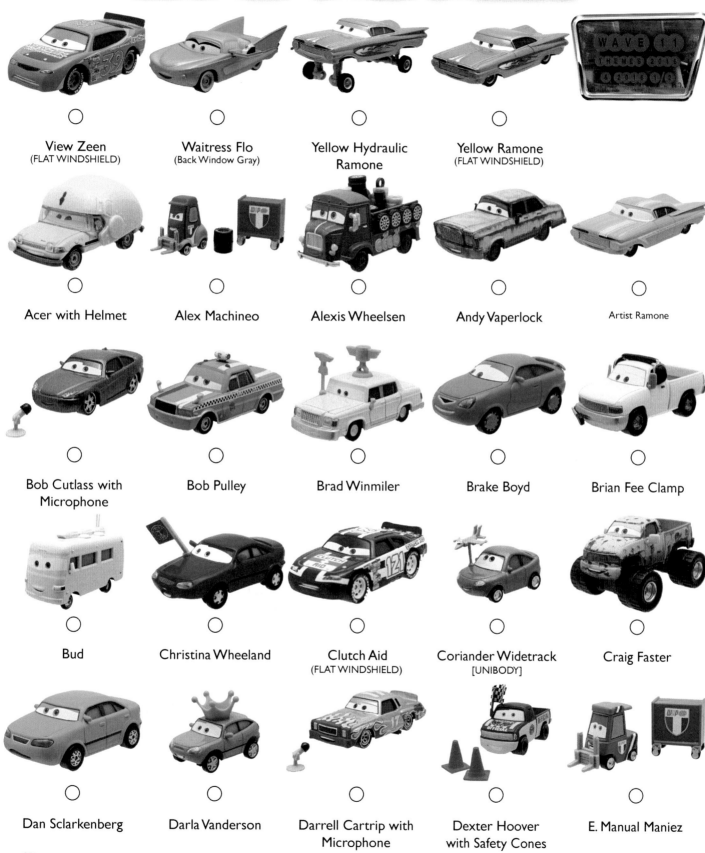

View Zeen
(FLAT WINDSHIELD)

Waitress Flo
(Back Window Gray)

Yellow Hydraulic
Ramone

Yellow Ramone
(FLAT WINDSHIELD)

Acer with Helmet

Alex Machineo

Alexis Wheelsen

Andy Vaperlock

Artist Ramone

Bob Cutlass with
Microphone

Bob Pulley

Brad Winmiler

Brake Boyd

Brian Fee Clamp

Bud

Christina Wheeland

Clutch Aid
(FLAT WINDSHIELD)

Coriander Widetrack
[UNIBODY]

Craig Faster

Dan Sclarkenberg

Darla Vanderson

Darrell Cartrip with
Microphone

Dexter Hoover
with Safety Cones

E. Manual Maniez

CARS are not necessarily in size or scale to each other. They are re-sized for grid conformity.
Double check circles indicate minor variant release that year. SEGMENTED or UNIBODY indicates first release of that production variant.

33

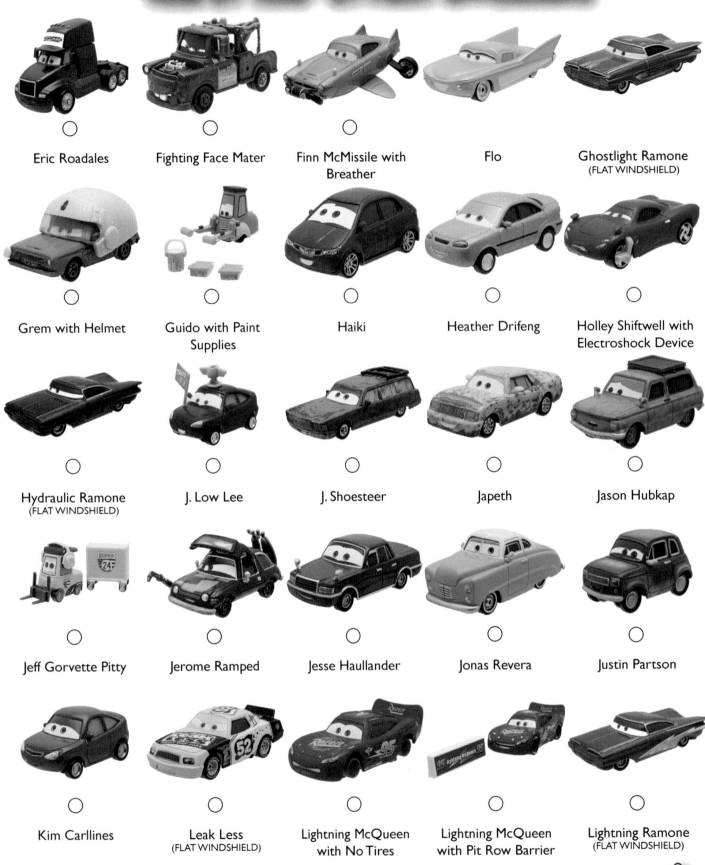

Eric Roadales	Fighting Face Mater	Finn McMissile with Breather	Flo	Ghostlight Ramone (FLAT WINDSHIELD)
Grem with Helmet	Guido with Paint Supplies	Haiki	Heather Drifeng	Holley Shiftwell with Electroshock Device
Hydraulic Ramone (FLAT WINDSHIELD)	J. Low Lee	J. Shoesteer	Japeth	Jason Hubkap
Jeff Gorvette Pitty	Jerome Ramped	Jesse Haullander	Jonas Revera	Justin Partson
Kim Carllines	Leak Less (FLAT WINDSHIELD)	Lightning McQueen with No Tires	Lightning McQueen with Pit Row Barrier	Lightning Ramone (FLAT WINDSHIELD)

CARS are not necessarily in size or scale to each other. They are re-sized for grid conformity.
Double check circles indicate minor variant release that year. SEGMENTED or UNIBODY indicates first release of that production variant.

Take5aDay.com

Lightning Storm McQueen (UNIBODY)

Lil' Torquey Pistons (FLAT WINDSHIELD)

Lizzie with Radio

M.A. Brake Drumm

Mater with Balloon

Mater with Duct Tape

Mater with No Tires

Max Schnell Kitty

Michael Sparkber

Michelle Motoretta

Mood Springs (FLAT WINDSHIELD)

Nitroade (FLAT WINDSHIELD)

Octane Gain (FLAT WINDSHIELD)

Old School Ramone (FLAT WINDSHIELD)

Otto Bonn

Paint Job Ramone

Percy Hanbrakes

Retread (FLAT WINDSHIELD)

Rev n Go (FLAT WINDSHIELD)

Re-Volting (FLAT WINDSHIELD)

Sedanya Oskanian

Shiny Wax with Pit Stop Barrier

Sidewall Shine with Pit Stop Barrier

Snot Rod (Hood Scoop Variant)

Sputter Stop (FLAT WINDSHIELD)

CARS are not necessarily in size or scale to each other. They are re-sized for grid conformity.
Double check circles indicate minor variant release that year. SEGMENTED or UNIBODY indicates first release of that production variant.

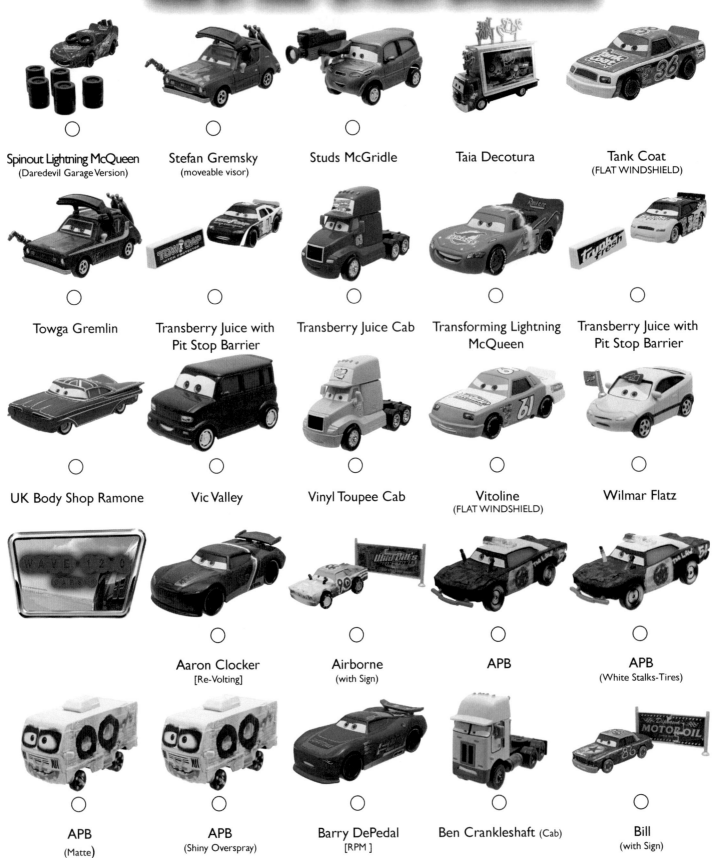

Spinout Lightning McQueen
(Daredevil Garage Version)

Stefan Gremsky
(moveable visor)

Studs McGridle

Taia Decotura

Tank Coat
(FLAT WINDSHIELD)

Towga Gremlin

Transberry Juice with
Pit Stop Barrier

Transberry Juice Cab

Transforming Lightning
McQueen

Transberry Juice with
Pit Stop Barrier

UK Body Shop Ramone

Vic Valley

Vinyl Toupee Cab

Vitoline
(FLAT WINDSHIELD)

Wilmar Flatz

Aaron Clocker
[Re-Volting]

Airborne
(with Sign)

APB

APB
(White Stalks-Tires)

APB
(Matte)

APB
(Shiny Overspray)

Barry DePedal
[RPM]

Ben Crankleshaft (Cab)

Bill
(with Sign)

CARS are not necessarily in size or scale to each other. They are re-sized for grid conformity.
Double check circles indicate minor variant release that year. SEGMENTED or UNIBODY indicates first release of that production variant.

Take5aDay.com

Blindspot

Bling Bling Lightning McQueen

Bobby Swift
[Octane Gain]

Brick Yardley
[Vitoline]

Broadside

Bruce Miller
[RPM]

Bubba Wheelhouse
[Transberry Juice]

Buck Bearingly
[View Zeen]

Cactus Lightning McQueen
(FLAT WINDSHIELD)

Cal Weathers
[Dinoco]

Cal "Hank" Weathers
(Incorrect Name on Roof)

CARS 3 Lightning McQueen

CARS 3 Lightning McQueen

CARS 3 Lightning McQueen

CARS 3 Mack

Chase Racelott
[Vitoline]

Chet Boxkaar Cab

Chick Hicks with Headset

Chip Bearings
[Combustr]

Cigalert

Cruz Ramirez

Cruz Ramirez as Frances Beltline

Cruz Ramirez as Frances Beltline (No Windshield Line)

Cruz Ramirez as Crazy 8 Frances Beltline

Danny Swervez
(Blue) [Octane Gain]

CARS are not necessarily in size or scale to each other. They are re-sized for grid conformity.
Double check circles indicate minor variant release that year. SEGMENTED or UNIBODY indicates first release of that production variant.

Danny Swervez
(Purple Tint) [Octane Gain]

Darren Leadfoot
[Shiny Wax]

Dinoco Cruz Ramirez
(Correct Window Supports)

Dinoco Cruz Ramirez
(No Window Supports)

Dirkson D'Agostino
[Trunk Fresh]

**Guido with Rust-Eze
Racing Center Tool Chest**

Herb Curbler
[Faux Wheel Drive]

Heyday Smokey

High Impact

Hit

HJ Hollis
[N20 Cola]

Jack DePost
[Tow Cap]

Jackson Storm
(Correct Window Supports)

Jackson Storm
(No Window Supports)

**Jackson Storm
with Piston Cup**

Jambalaya Chimichanga
(with Tires)

JD McPillar
[Tow Cap]

Jeff Gorvette CARS 3

Jerry Recycled Battery
(Cab)

Jimbo

Jimmy Cables
[Intersection]

Junior Moon

Kris Revstopski

Liability
(with Tires)

Lane Locke
[SynerG]

CARS are not necessarily in size or scale to each other. They are re-sized for grid conformity.
Double check circles indicate minor variant release that year. SEGMENTED or UNIBODY indicates first release of that production variant.

○	○	○	○	○
Lightning McQueen as Chester Whipplefilter	Lightning McQueen as Chester Whipplefilter	Lightning McQ as Chester Whipplefilter (with Barrels)	Louise Nash	Luigi with Flag
○	○	○	○	○
Luigi with Hay Bales	Maddy McGear	Making of CARS 3 Lightning [#1 Zamack]	Making of CARS 3 Lightning [#2 Red Coat]	Making of CARS 3 Lightning [#3 Metallic]
○	○	○	○	○
Miss Fritter (Correct Stop Sign - Matte)	Miss Fritter (Incorrect Stop Sign)	Morgan Martins	Mr. Drippy	Murry Clutchburn [Sputter Stop]
○	○	○	○	○
Natalie Certain	Parker Brakeston [N20 Cola]	Pat Traxson	Patty (Black Roof)	Patty (Gray Roof)
○	○	○	○	○
Paul Conrev [Bumper Save]	Paul valdez Cab	Phil Tankson [Nitroade]	Pileup	Ponchy Wipeout (Black Rims)

CARS are not necessarily in size or scale to each other. They are re-sized for grid conformity.
Double check circles indicate minor variant release that year. SEGMENTED or UNIBODY indicates first release of that production variant.

39

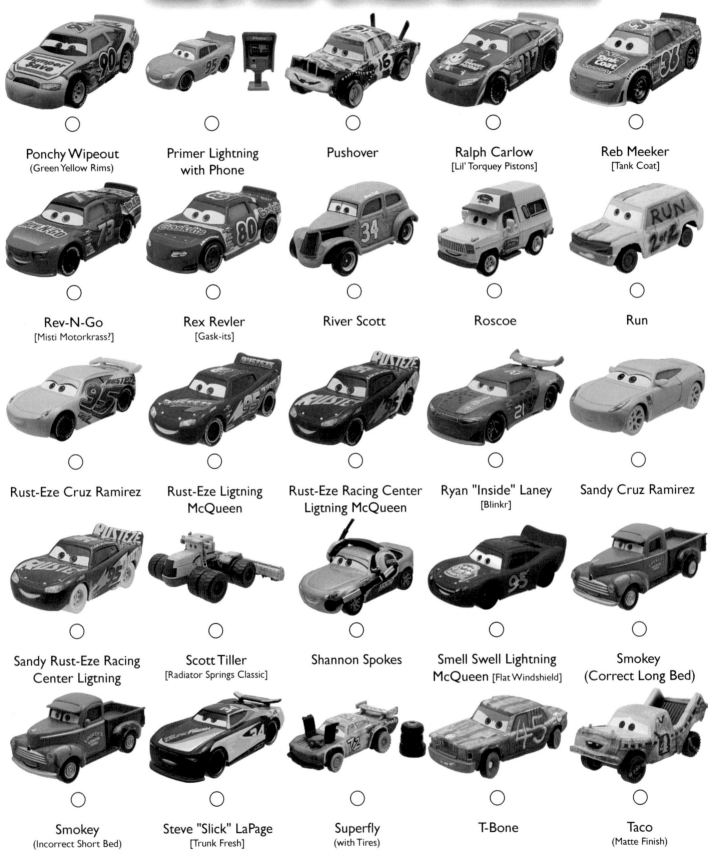

Ponchy Wipeout (Green Yellow Rims)	Primer Lightning with Phone	Pushover	Ralph Carlow [Lil' Torquey Pistons]	Reb Meeker [Tank Coat]
Rev-N-Go [Misti Motorkrass?]	Rex Revler [Gask-its]	River Scott	Roscoe	Run
Rust-Eze Cruz Ramirez	Rust-Eze Ligtning McQueen	Rust-Eze Racing Center Ligtning McQueen	Ryan "Inside" Laney [Blinkr]	Sandy Cruz Ramirez
Sandy Rust-Eze Racing Center Ligtning	Scott Tiller [Radiator Springs Classic]	Shannon Spokes	Smell Swell Lightning McQueen [Flat Windshield]	Smokey (Correct Long Bed)
Smokey (Incorrect Short Bed)	Steve "Slick" LaPage [Trunk Fresh]	Superfly (with Tires)	T-Bone	Taco (Matte Finish)

CARS are not necessarily in size or scale to each other. They are re-sized for grid conformity.
Double check circles indicate minor variant release that year. SEGMENTED or UNIBODY indicates first release of that production variant.

Taco
(Shiny Overspray)

Tailgate

Terry Kargas
[Triple Dent]

Tim Treadless
[Nitroade]

Tiny Lugsworth

Todd
("Clean")

Todd Marcus
[No Stall]

Tommy Highbanks
[Faux Wheel Drive]

Tongue Lightning
McQueen [Flat Windshield]

Tractor (V2 - Eye Position)
[Radiator Springs Classic]

Tumbleweed Lightning
McQueen [Flat Windshield]

Van
(Dirty Cargo Carrier Variant)

Ben Crankleshaft

Bobby Swift Hauler
(Blue)

Bobby Swift Hauler
(Incorrect Purple)

Bumper Save

Cal Weathers Hauler
(Also variant with light blue cap)

CARS 3 Mack Hauler

Chet Boxkaar

Chick Hauler

Gil

Gray - Dinoco

Jerry Recycled
Batteries

Jocko Flocko Mack
Hauler

CARS are not necessarily in size or scale to each other. They are re-sized for grid conformity.
Double check circles indicate minor variant release that year. SEGMENTED or UNIBODY indicates first release of that production variant.

41

Mack

Mack
(CARS 2)

Mood Springs

Nitroade

No Stall

Octane Gain

Oliver Lightload

Paul Valdez

Road Trippin' Mack

RPM

Shifty Drug

Sidewall Shine

Trunk Fresh

Vinyl Toupee

Wally Hauler

Darrell Cartrip

Fillmore

Finn McMissile

Francesco Bernoulli

Holley Shiftwell

Lightning McQueen

Mater

Miles Axelrod

Professor Z

CARS are not necessarily in size or scale to each other. They are re-sized for grid conformity.
Double check circles indicate minor variant release that year. SEGMENTED or UNIBODY indicates first release of that production variant.

Take 5 aDay.com

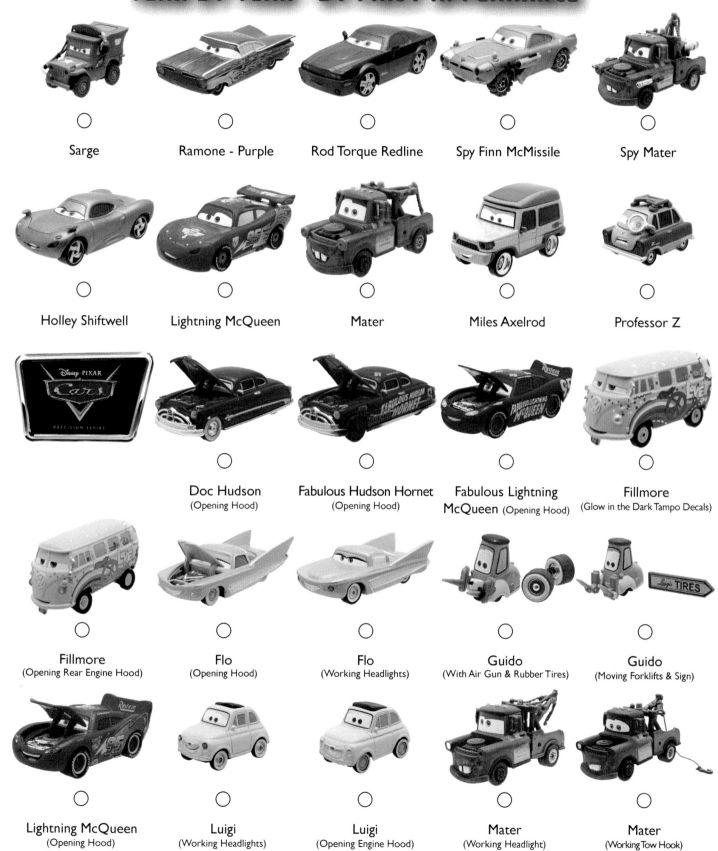

Sarge

Ramone - Purple

Rod Torque Redline

Spy Finn McMissile

Spy Mater

Holley Shiftwell

Lightning McQueen

Mater

Miles Axelrod

Professor Z

Doc Hudson
(Opening Hood)

Fabulous Hudson Hornet
(Opening Hood)

Fabulous Lightning
McQueen (Opening Hood)

Fillmore
(Glow in the Dark Tampo Decals)

Fillmore
(Opening Rear Engine Hood)

Flo
(Opening Hood)

Flo
(Working Headlights)

Guido
(With Air Gun & Rubber Tires)

Guido
(Moving Forklifts & Sign)

Lightning McQueen
(Opening Hood)

Luigi
(Working Headlights)

Luigi
(Opening Engine Hood)

Mater
(Working Headlight)

Mater
(Working Tow Hook)

CARS are not necessarily in size or scale to each other. They are re-sized for grid conformity.
Double check circles indicate minor variant release that year. SEGMENTED or UNIBODY indicates first release of that production variant.

43

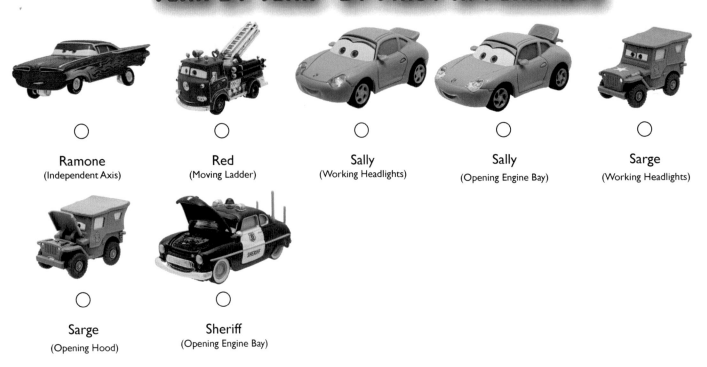

Ramone
(Independent Axis)

Red
(Moving Ladder)

Sally
(Working Headlights)

Sally
(Opening Engine Bay)

Sarge
(Working Headlights)

Sarge
(Opening Hood)

Sheriff
(Opening Engine Bay)

DESERT ART - it all started so simple. A handful of releases, a small refresh and probably a few more releases when the DVD-VHS came out (VHS? Yes, it's been that long) but after that, maybe some holiday box set releases but like every other licensed movie, the thinking was that this line would lose consumer interest quickly. But no one knew. The movie touched the kid in all of us and Mattel did an amazing job in bringing the now beloved characters to life. From April 2006 to October 2006, they kept re-releasing the same 28 singles and 2-packs, & box sets and people kept stripping the shelves bare. Lizzie ended up with countless variants - her first release featured a short front axle plate - all subsequent releases feature a larger plate. Her radiator cap has changed shape from a squarish lump to a round shape AND there are versions where the radiator cap is below and above the radiator. Is there a definitive "correct" release? No, one really knows. Mattel ultimately settled on a round radiator cap above the radiator hood line with a large axle plate. And while there are also error ones with white lights, her headlamps should be purple.

SUPERCHARGED - The card switchover was in November 2006 - Unlike other diecast or licensed lines, all the previous CARS diecasts were re-released (making everyone but the hoarders happy - though they had new cards to collect) along with a few new sculpts. While a slew of new sculpts were shown off at ToyFair, the second wave didn't really arrive until late Spring. Case information was now regularly available (unlike Hot Wheels) but as the cases hit retail, they were still an instant sellout. Then the recall of Sarge hit (high lead content). Since Target and Walmart sells by master SKU's - they didn't bother to seek out just Sarge but quarantined the entire CARS SKU's. And Mattel stopped shipping. But by the end of summer of 2007, the first exclusives at Walmart hit (the WM 8 cards) and it was time to transition to the next motif.

WORLD OF CARS - Every previous release (except for variant fixes and recalled Sarge) was re-released, the last year this happened as the line grew too large. It was also the year of the Motor Speedway of the South set. It was the first year of launchers, deluxe oversized, the first SDCC exclusive, and mail-aways. It was the golden age of CARS collecting. Cases were released every 2-3 weeks, minor issues aside, new CARS diecasts generally were shipped 2-4 in a case and each of the Big 4 retailers got cases in on a regular basis - all you had to do was drive around to complete your collection. This and the next year were the Golden Age of CARS Collecting.

The Kmart CARS Day event started - what could be better? Simply show up to buy exclusive CARS. But as with every Golden Age - it shines brightly and then dims.

44

CARS are not necessarily in size or scale to each other. They are re-sized for grid conformity.
Double check circles indicate minor variant release that year. SEGMENTED or UNIBODY indicates first release of that production variant.

RACE O RAMA - While not every diecast was re-released, most were - Race O Rama witnessed the first haulers, the first chase CARS and more of the rubber tire racers at Kmart. There were now 200+ different sculpts after 4 years. It was the continuation of the golden age of CARS collecting. Depth. Breath. Easy availability at retail. (Plus Toons). The Golden Age then ended abruptly in the Summer of 2009. In the first of many puzzling decisions, Mattel decided to split the line. Target Stores got the classic fixed eyes "Final Lap Series." All other retailers got the "lenticular" CARS with eyes that moved. As with many plans in this line, it's not so much the decision but the execution. Instead of an even distribution of the Final Lap releases, some diecasts got multiple releases while others received limited distribution especially towards the end of 2009.

So, as the classic fix eye releases were now Target only exclusives - all other retailers got the lenticular releases and re-releases. This was also the era of high commodity costs so many diecasts were re-designed with a segmented face plate (plastic) which not only saved costs but in theory, offered greater expression flexibility (you didn't need a new mold to change expressions). As a result, 22 diecasts ended up as unique with both a lenticular windshield AND a segmented face plate - so if you're a variant collector, you might want to add those to your list - these are diecasts that were previously never released as segmented such as Cruisin' Lightning McQueen, Chuki, etc ... (see the "segmented" lenticular starting on page 14).

LENTICULAR RACE O RAMA - The first wave consisted of ONLY common re-releases (see Page 14). May 2009 to September 2009. These tended to feature lenticular eyebrows that opened and closed.

LENTICULAR NIGHT SKYLINE - New releases were folded into the mix but virtually all of the "new" releases were also available as Target's Final Lap (with classic fix eyes) EXCEPT for the CHASE series which were now ONLY lenticular. October 2009 to October 2010. There were 32 unique releases including CHASES though some variants with segmented faces with no equivalent classic fixed-eye releases. The "Night Skyline" lenticular tended to feature eyes that moved from left to right.

FINAL LAP/NIGHT SKYLINE - September 2008 for Final Lap, then the Night Skyline motif until early 2010. The Final Lap was great in that in a short burst, over 60 new singles were released. The problem again was the wildly uneven retail distribution. Some diecasts were over shipped, others arrived once and never returned. Art of Rolling CARS. Yes. Business plan? One that even a communist would reject. And to add to the confusion, all other releases (Deluxe, box sets, launchers, Toons and other Expanded Universe were ALL fixed-eye releases) available at all stores.

PORTO CORSA (CARS 2) - Without repeating every detail of the nightmare of CARS 2 distribution and planning (see our checklist issue #9), it lasted 18 months so in about 78 weeks, the first 2 weeks of Porto Corsa were fine and the last 2 were nice. In between, a long strange trip in an upside down Submarine Finn McMissile. The problem was not the (over) commitment of retailers for CARS 2 but rather the poor mix of the first 4 cases. As there were only 20 new releases in the mix of the first cases, retail stores were wildly overstocked. Because CARS 2 LM, Mater, Francesco & Finn were packed in multiples in each of the early cases AND with stores getting up to 10+ cases, some of these 4 hung around on the shelves for nearly TWO years! Each new release (short packed) were quickly sold out, leaving the 4 to continually gather dust giving retailers who only track by a master SKU the impression sales were slow when even new collectors would only buy so many of the initial 4 characters. There was an attempt to switch over to a London Theme but with so many singles still on the shelf and poor re-ordering, Porto Corsa ended up the longest theme motif at retail - nearly a year-and-a-half before finally being replaced. The theme lasted so long that many segmented face releases were upgraded and released with all-metal unbodies by the end of its run.

THEMES 2013 to 2016/2016 1/2 - Finally in 2013, a switch to a new motif. Diecast characters were grouped by a sub-theme such as the CARS 2 racers under a "WGP" banner and numbered within that group such as 2 of 12. Themes 2013 also brought a return to CARS 1 diecasts returning and many obscure characters finally getting a release.

This "Themes" motif continued through April 2017 (before CARS 3) While the themes banners changed from year to year, most collectors ignored the banners and collected by the diecasts they wanted. There was a great variety of fun, obscure CARS 2 characters and thought to be forgotten CARS characters. Again, distribution was weak but the sculpts and releases were great - boding well for the release of CARS 3.

There were quite a few re-releases that actually went back to an all-metal unibody or interestedly enough, a diecast that was first released with a segmented face got that replaced with a unibody! A very nice upgrade. On the other hand, most of the early characters that had a raised metal eyebrow got those replaced with a painted one (designated in the guide as "flat windshield").

CARS are not necessarily in size or scale to each other. They are re-sized for grid conformity.
Double check circles indicate minor variant release that year. SEGMENTED or UNIBODY indicates first release of that production variant.

45

CARS 3 - A much better distribution but still wanting but much better and smoother. There were 133 new releases from CARS 3! A great range of revised Piston Cup racers, Next Gen racers, Thunder Hollow demolition derby "wrecked" CARS, old racers and even Deluxe vehicles with moving parts!

RADIATOR SPRINGS CLASSIC (TRU Only) - A TRU only card/motif that featured only CARS 1 re-releases with few production change so they are not listed separately. In 2015, we got a variant Tar LM (Flat windshield) and a "new" release, Hydraulic Yellow Ramone - all others were re-releases. 2018 actually started well with a mix of RS townies with new expressions plus a few new releases + a brand new Deluxe character from CARS 3 but as Toy R Us closed up its doors in 2018, this line is up in the air. The 2018 are not included here yet.

HAULERS - 23 releases. And only 15 of the 36 Piston Cup racer haulers from CARS 1 have been released. There is only 1 release from CARS 2 with Mack's new artwork. The first addition of an Expanded Universe release was from the Road Trip Series - Road Trippin' Mack. There were 5 new releases from CARS 3 including the first variant.

DISNEY STORE - 12 releases that are in scale - mostly characters not available from Mattel but a few repeats. The THEME PARK (StarWars) CARS Wars are listed separately. While there were CARS 3 releases at the Disney Store, none were characters in-scale to the Mattel 1:55 series so nothing new has been added.

The Toons-Storytellers-Expanded Universe gets complicated. In the initial phase of release of the "Expanded Universe" diecasts, it was relatively simple. There were Mater Tall Tales shorts from Pixar (thus canon) and diecast releases to match. There were a series of official books that explained how the characters arrived in Radiator Springs (WORLD OF CARS) and holiday themed books (MATER SAVES CHRISTMAS & MATER & THE EASTER BUGGY). However, CARS 2, it's gotten complicated as while the "Protect & Serve," diecasts were released, the Toon while announced has never aired AND there were a series of CARS WGP racers released as international race vehicles. While the NEON RACERS got a very limited release book - none of the other race diecast releases were "made canon," with a book but since they are all re-paints of the racers, everything released by Mattel is under the Expanded Universe canon in some manner or another.

TOONS - In 2008 and 2009, we got nearly 100 releases along with the regular mainline. After then, it has slowed to a trickle but we have added another 40+ Toon diecasts including great ones from the Time Travel Mater, Radiator Springs 500 1/2 and to Protect & Serve shorts. Re-releases have returned as a WM only exclusive - with a few new ones and a few unibody upgrades. While the 2016 Road Trip Series is not really a Toon (no short or book) but since they feature the main townies, they are counted here.

STORYTELLERS - The first releases were directly related to the book that filled in the back story of how the characters arrived in Radiator Springs. The Christmas releases also fall under this umbrella as the book is marked. However, since then, the releases based on books are not listed as "storytellers" such as the Easter Buggy book diecasts released in 2016. In 2018, we got the first Holiday Sarge & a Mater variant in 2017.

EXPANDED UNIVERSE - All of the WGP racers series have been folded into this umbrella: Carbon Racers; Carnival Cup Racers; Ice Racers & Neon Racers. While there was a book for the "Neon Racers" race, there is no supporting material for the other races - though they are clearly repaints of CARS 2 characters.

LIGHTS & SOUNDS - There were 14 nice releases for CARS 2 of the main diecasts with lights & sounds. Only Professor Z is out of scale to get in the electronics and batteries - the others look essentially like the regular 1:55 releases. Each vehicle was activated with a button with sounds or dialogue from the film. The voices seem to be the original voice actors' - other than Owen as Lightning, that might be a secondary voice actor.

PRECISION SERIES - With the announcement of the entire town playsets upgraded to lights and accurate scale, singles and vehicles included with playsets were upgraded in production quality and functional features (opening hood/trunks) or working headlamps. Counting singles and diecasts included with the playsets, we have 25 releases so far.

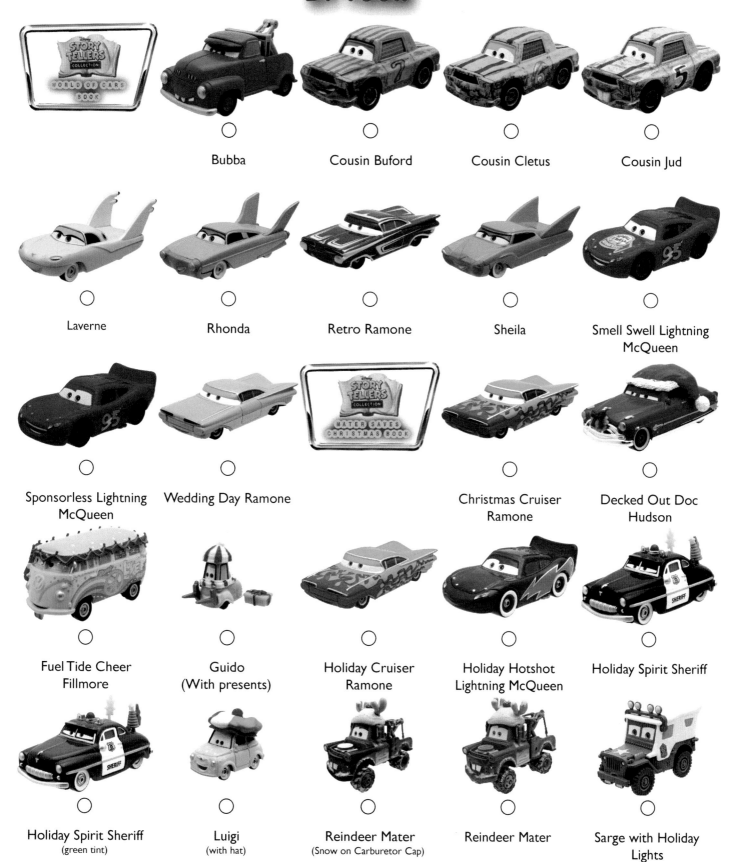

| | Bubba | Cousin Buford | Cousin Cletus | Cousin Jud |

| Laverne | Rhonda | Retro Ramone | Sheila | Smell Swell Lightning McQueen |

| Sponsorless Lightning McQueen | Wedding Day Ramone | | Christmas Cruiser Ramone | Decked Out Doc Hudson |

| Fuel Tide Cheer Fillmore | Guido (With presents) | Holiday Cruiser Ramone | Holiday Hotshot Lightning McQueen | Holiday Spirit Sheriff |

| Holiday Spirit Sheriff (green tint) | Luigi (with hat) | Reindeer Mater (Snow on Carburetor Cap) | Reindeer Mater | Sarge with Holiday Lights |

Take5aDay.com

CARS are not necessarily in size or scale to each other. They are re-sized for grid conformity.
Double check circles indicate minor variant release that year. SEGMENTED or UNIBODY indicates first release of that production variant.

47

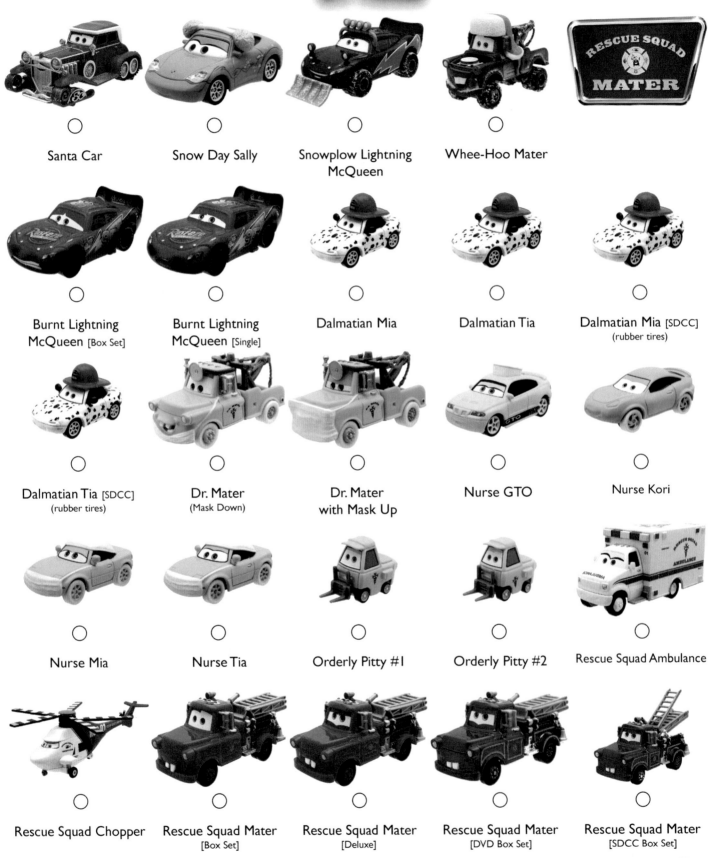

Santa Car

Snow Day Sally

Snowplow Lightning McQueen

Whee-Hoo Mater

Burnt Lightning McQueen [Box Set]

Burnt Lightning McQueen [Single]

Dalmatian Mia

Dalmatian Tia

Dalmatian Mia [SDCC] (rubber tires)

Dalmatian Tia [SDCC] (rubber tires)

Dr. Mater (Mask Down)

Dr. Mater with Mask Up

Nurse GTO

Nurse Kori

Nurse Mia

Nurse Tia

Orderly Pitty #1

Orderly Pitty #2

Rescue Squad Ambulance

Rescue Squad Chopper

Rescue Squad Mater [Box Set]

Rescue Squad Mater [Deluxe]

Rescue Squad Mater [DVD Box Set]

Rescue Squad Mater [SDCC Box Set]

48

CARS are not necessarily in size or scale to each other. They are re-sized for grid conformity.
Double check circles indicate minor variant release that year. SEGMENTED or UNIBODY indicates first release of that production variant.

Rescue Squad Trooper

Rescue Squad Trooper
(Error grill)

Soaked Lightning
McQueen

Big Fan

Buck Tooth Vendor

Bucky Brakedust

Cannonball Mater

Daredevil McQueen

Daredevil McQueen
with Teeth (UNIBODY)

Daredevil McQueen
with Teeth (segmented)

Fan Mia

Fan Tia

High Dive Mater

Lug
[Single]

Lug
[Aviator Box set]

Lug
[Daredevil Box set]

Lug
[Sign Box set]

Lug with Oil Cans

Mater the Aviator

Mater the Greater

Nutty
[Single]

Nutty
[Sign Box set]

Nutty with Oil Cans

Props McGee

CARS are not necessarily in size or scale to each other. They are re-sized for grid conformity.
Double check circles indicate minor variant release that year. SEGMENTED or UNIBODY indicates first release of that production variant.

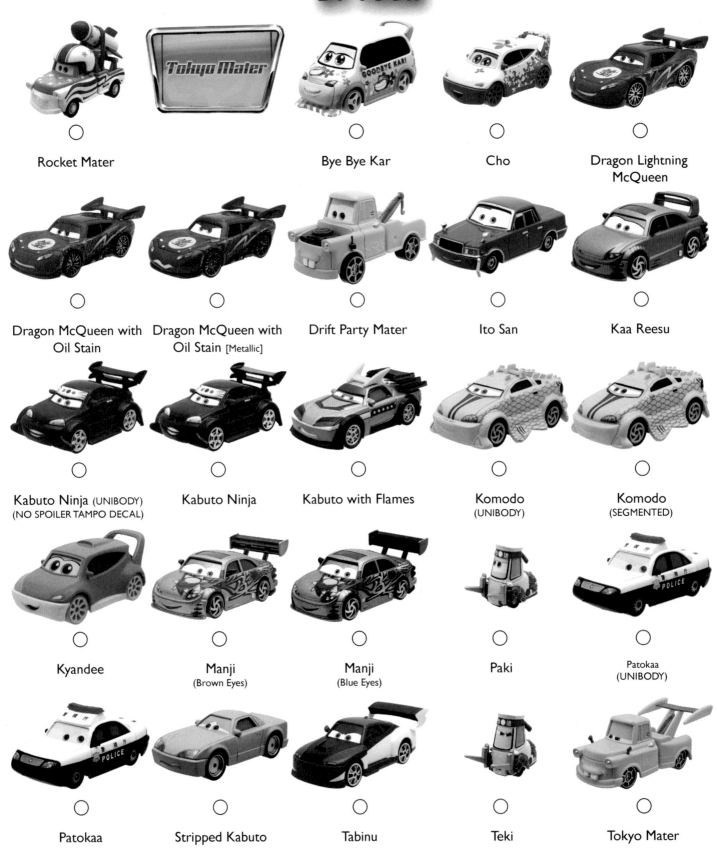

Rocket Mater

Bye Bye Kar

Cho

Dragon Lightning McQueen

Dragon McQueen with Oil Stain

Dragon McQueen with Oil Stain [Metallic]

Drift Party Mater

Ito San

Kaa Reesu

Kabuto Ninja (UNIBODY) (NO SPOILER TAMPO DECAL)

Kabuto Ninja

Kabuto with Flames

Komodo (UNIBODY)

Komodo (SEGMENTED)

Kyandee

Manji (Brown Eyes)

Manji (Blue Eyes)

Paki

Patokaa (UNIBODY)

Patokaa

Stripped Kabuto

Tabinu

Teki

Tokyo Mater

CARS are not necessarily in size or scale to each other. They are re-sized for grid conformity.
Double check circles indicate minor variant release that year. SEGMENTED or UNIBODY indicates first release of that production variant.

Tokyo Mater with Flames [SDCC]

Tokyo Mater with Oil Stains

Van San

Yojimbo

MONSTER TRUCK MATER

Beanie Mater

Dr. Feel Bad

Frightening McMean [Box Set #1]

Frightening McMean [Box Set #2]

Frightening McMean [Box Set #3]

I-Screamer

I-Screamer's Biggest Fan

Rasta Carian

Rasta Mater

Ref with Bell

Tormentor

Tormentor's Biggest Fan

UFM — UNIDENTIFIED FLYING MATER

Captain Munier

Corporal Kim

Dr. Abschlepp Wagen

Mator the UFO

EL MATERDOR

Chuy

El Materdor (Int'l only release)

Take5aDay.com

CARS are not necessarily in size or scale to each other. They are re-sized for grid conformity.
Double check circles indicate minor variant release that year. SEGMENTED or UNIBODY indicates first release of that production variant.

51

Padre

Dex

Eddie

Heavy Metal Lightning
McQueen

Heavy Metal Mater

Music Video Mater

Rocky

Rodney the Rocker

Autonaut Lightning
McQueen

Autonaut Mater

Burnt Autonaut
Lightning McQueen

NASCA Truck

Stu Bop the Jet

Aviator Mater

Falcon Hawk I

Falcon Hawk Black

Lightning Hawk

Lightning Hawk
[Metallic]

Mater Hawk

Mater Hawk
[Metallic]

Propwash Junction
Biplane

Rescue Chopper

52

CARS are not necessarily in size or scale to each other. They are re-sized for grid conformity.
Double check circles indicate minor variant release that year. SEGMENTED or UNIBODY indicates first release of that production variant.

Time Travel Mater

○ Time Travel Lightning McQueen

○ Time Travel Mater

○ Time Travel Stanley

○ Wedding Day Lizzie

○ Wedding Day Stanley

The RADIATOR SPRINGS 500½ AN EXCLUSIVE PIXAR SHORT

○ Blue Grit

○ Off-Road Lightning McQueen

○ Off-Road Mater

○ Sandy Dunes

○ Shifty Sidewinder

○ Stanley Days Fillmore

○ Stanley Days Ramone

○ Stanley Days Sarge

Tales from RADIATOR SPRINGS

○ Rad. Springs Team McQueen (Smaller Lighter Tampo Decals)

○ Rad. Springs Team McQueen (Larger, Darker Tampo Decals)

○

○ Didi 05

○ Driving School Lightning McQueen

○ Mike 07

CARBON RACERS

○

○ Carbon Racer Carla Veloso

○ Carbon Racer Francesco Bernoulli

CARS are not necessarily in size or scale to each other. They are re-sized for grid conformity.
Double check circles indicate minor variant release that year. SEGMENTED or UNIBODY indicates first release of that production variant.

53

○ Carbon Racer Frosty
(Australia Exclusive)

○ Carbon Racer
Jeff Gorvette

○ Carbon Racer
Lewis Hamilton

○ Carbon Racer
Lightning McQueen

○ Carbon Racer
Max Schnell

○ Carbon Racer
Miguel Camino

○ Carbon Racer
Nigel Gearsley

○ Carbon Racer
Raoul Caroule

○ Carbon Racer
Shu Todoroki

○ Carnival Racer
Carla Veloso

○ Carnival Racer
Francisco Bernoulli

○ Carnival Racer
Jeff Gorvette

○ Carnival Racer
Lewis Hamilton

○ Carnival Racer
Lightning McQueen

○ Carnival Racer
Lightning McQueen

○ Carnival Racer
Max Schnell

○ Carnival Racer
Miguel Camino

○ Carnival Racer
Nigel Gearsley

○ Carnival Racer
Raoul Caroule

○ Carnival Racer
Rip Cllutchgoneski

○ Carnival Racer
Shu Todoroki

○ Easter Buggy

○ Easter Lightning
McQueen

CARS are not necessarily in size or scale to each other. They are re-sized for grid conformity.
Double check circles indicate minor variant release that year. SEGMENTED or UNIBODY indicates first release of that production variant.

Take 5 aDay.com

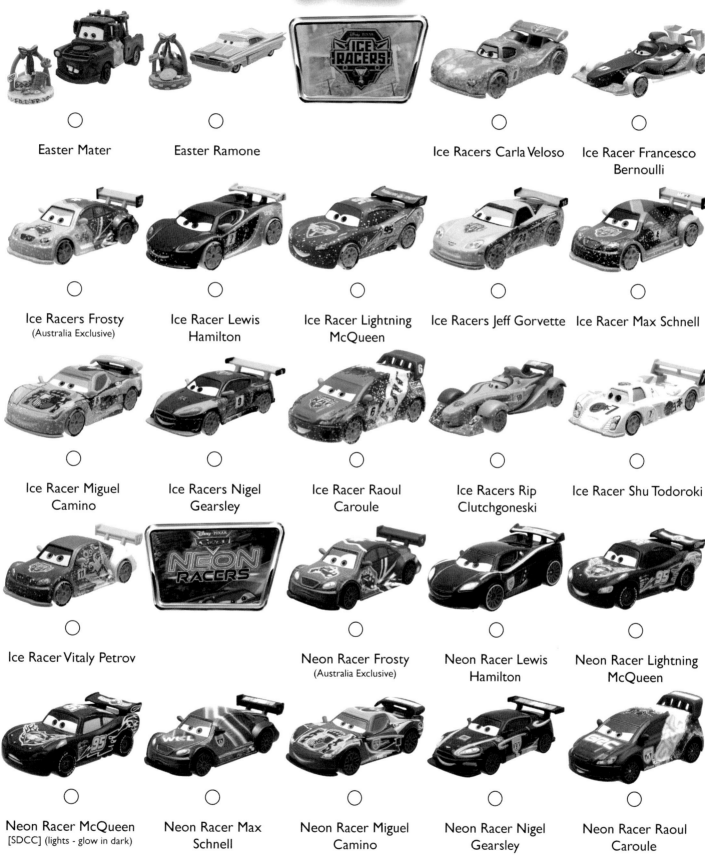

Easter Mater

Easter Ramone

Ice Racers Carla Veloso

Ice Racer Francesco Bernoulli

Ice Racers Frosty
(Australia Exclusive)

Ice Racer Lewis Hamilton

Ice Racer Lightning McQueen

Ice Racers Jeff Gorvette

Ice Racer Max Schnell

Ice Racer Miguel Camino

Ice Racers Nigel Gearsley

Ice Racer Raoul Caroule

Ice Racers Rip Clutchgoneski

Ice Racer Shu Todoroki

Ice Racer Vitaly Petrov

Neon Racer Frosty
(Australia Exclusive)

Neon Racer Lewis Hamilton

Neon Racer Lightning McQueen

Neon Racer McQueen
[SDCC] (lights - glow in dark)

Neon Racer Max Schnell

Neon Racer Miguel Camino

Neon Racer Nigel Gearsley

Neon Racer Raoul Caroule

CARS are not necessarily in size or scale to each other. They are re-sized for grid conformity.
Double check circles indicate minor variant release that year. SEGMENTED or UNIBODY indicates first release of that production variant.

○	○		○	○
Neon Racer Shu Todoroki	Neon Racer Todoroki [SDCC] (lights - glow in dark)		Road Trip Cruisin' Lightning McQueen	Road Trip Cruisin' McQueen & Trailer
○	○	○	○	○
Road Trip Fillmore	Road Trip Fillmore & Trailer	Road Trip Flo	Road Trip Mater	Road Trip Mater & Trailer
○	○	○	○	○
Road Trip Red & Wagon	Road Trip Ramone & Trailer	Road Trip Sally	Road Trip Sarge	Road Trip Sarge & Trailer
○	○	○	○	○
Road Trip Sheriff & Trailer		Big D	Barmaid	Double Decker Bus
○	○	○	○	○
Frank	Goofy Mater	I-Screamer	Josh Coolant	Mickey Lightning McQueen

CARS are not necessarily in size or scale to each other. They are re-sized for grid conformity.
Double check circles indicate minor variant release that year. SEGMENTED or UNIBODY indicates first release of that production variant.

Take5aDay.com

MATTEL DISNEY PIXAR CARS |EXPANDED UNIVERSE & DISNEY
BY TOON

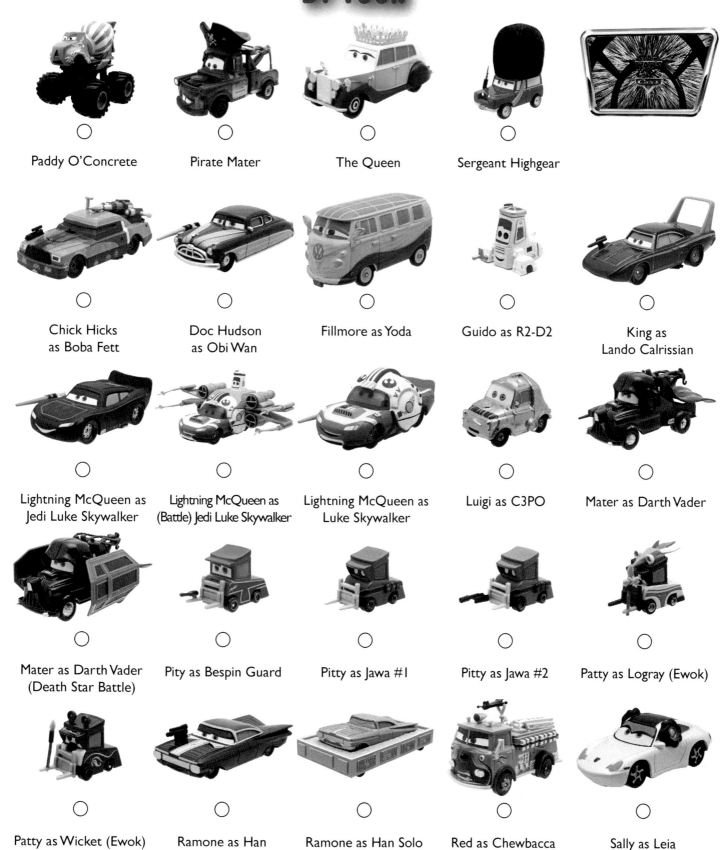

Paddy O'Concrete

Pirate Mater

The Queen

Sergeant Highgear

Chick Hicks
as Boba Fett

Doc Hudson
as Obi Wan

Fillmore as Yoda

Guido as R2-D2

King as
Lando Calrissian

Lightning McQueen as
Jedi Luke Skywalker

Lightning McQueen as
(Battle) Jedi Luke Skywalker

Lightning McQueen as
Luke Skywalker

Luigi as C3PO

Mater as Darth Vader

Mater as Darth Vader
(Death Star Battle)

Pity as Bespin Guard

Pitty as Jawa #1

Pitty as Jawa #2

Patty as Logray (Ewok)

Patty as Wicket (Ewok)

Ramone as Han

Ramone as Han Solo
Carbonite [Removable]

Red as Chewbacca

Sally as Leia

CARS are not necessarily in size or scale to each other. They are re-sized for grid conformity.
Double check circles indicate minor variant release that year. SEGMENTED or UNIBODY indicates first release of that production variant.

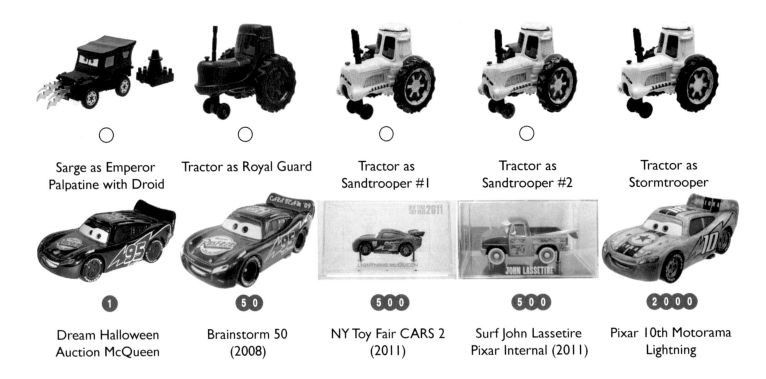

Sarge as Emperor Palpatine with Droid

Tractor as Royal Guard

Tractor as Sandtrooper #1

Tractor as Sandtrooper #2

Tractor as Stormtrooper

Dream Halloween Auction McQueen

Brainstorm 50 (2008)

NY Toy Fair CARS 2 (2011)

Surf John Lassetire Pixar Internal (2011)

Pixar 10th Motorama Lightning

These are the rarest of the promotional CARS diecasts that were not offered to the public. The numbers underneath indicate the production run - the Motorama is a guess. These are NOT counted in the checklists as the originals are very hard to find - though counterfeits abound.

The Dream Halloween Auction McQueen is ONE worldwide in a display case - last seen at TRU's headquarters in NJ.

The Brainstorm 50 was given to Mattel, Disney & Pixar employees at a CARS diecast brainstorm meeting in 2008 - it came with an entire gift bag so verify its authenticity! What's interesting is while there are hundreds if not thousands of counterfeits and usually referred to as "Ransburg Red," the color of these fakes are actually incorrect as these quickly made promotional CARS were done at a Mattel plant which uses the Mattel color process - so it's really Spectraflame Red which is more of an orange red and a color difficult to match since its Mattel's own proprietary process.

The Toy Fair CARS 2 was given to members of the press so its availability is possible though it is really just a retail CARS 2 LM drilled and mounted in an acrylic case.

The "surf" John Lassetire were given to the CARS 2 cast & crew. The diecast is not difficult to recreate and there are counterfeits but the acrylic box AND the outside cardboard box are not possible (or worthwhile to recreate) so if you are paying top dollar, make sure it comes with the acrylic case at least.

The Motorama diecast is an unpainted LM decoed for the 10th anniversary of Pixar's annual auto show.

There is one other CARS 2 promo car only for the Pixar film crew - NOT SHOWN - probably numbering in the 500 range. I have seen a photo but I have been asked not to reveal it unless another person reveals it (aka: showing up on eBay) - so far, after 5 years, none have appeared but I'd be happy to verify if it's the correct one - just drop us an email at TakeFiveADay.

58

CARS are not necessarily in size or scale to each other. They are re-sized for grid conformity.
Double check circles indicate minor variant release that year. SEGMENTED or UNIBODY indicates first release of that production variant.

After 12 years, it should be a smooth running operation but strangely, we have only had a few years of normalcy but mostly, it's been an endeavor to persevere.

So, what is the final count? Well, it's not a locked-in firm number because what is a worthy-significant production change and what isn't? That's totally subjective - adding a decal to the back spoiler is really a minor change but not when it's Lightning McQueen ... So the reality is everyone's number is different but here is the general yearly/motif and the "new" CARS diecast release count. There are some who are only collecting CARS 1 diecasts, others everything so here's the overall running total, you decide on your sliding scale on what to collect! Good luck!

MOTIF	NEW COUNT	RUNNING TOTAL
Desert Art	28	28
Supercharged 2.0 & 2.5	34	62
Supercharged WM 8	8	70
World of CARS	63	133
Race O Rama	71	204
Night Skyline/Final Lap	71	275
Lenticular CHASE	15	290
Lenticular Segmented Variants	22	312
Lenticular Race O Rama	9	321
Lenticular Night Skyline	60	381
Porto Corsa	129	510
Porto Corsa Silver Metallic	11	521
Themes 2013	79	600
Themes 2014	59	659
Themes 2015	67	726
Themes 2016	85	811
CARS 1 New (2017)	8	819
CARS 1 Variants (2017)	6	825
CARS 3	133	958
(Total Variants 2006-2017)	194	1,152
Haulers	28	1,180
Expanded Universe	93	1,273
Toons	144	1,417
Disney Store	12	1,429
Lights & Sounds	15	1,444
Precision Series	21	1,465
Rubber Tire CARS 1 & 2	44	**1,509**

Collect Them All!

DESERT ART SERIES
MATTEL DISNEY PIXAR CARS · VOLUME 1
WRITTEN BY: KC

SUPERCHARGED SERIES
MATTEL DISNEY PIXAR CARS · VOLUME 2
WRITTEN BY: KC

WORLD OF CARS SERIES
MATTEL DISNEY PIXAR CARS · VOLUME 3

RACE O RAMA SERIES
MATTEL DISNEY PIXAR CARS · VOLUME 4
WRITTEN BY: KC

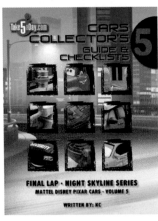

FINAL LAP · NIGHT SKYLINE SERIES
MATTEL DISNEY PIXAR CARS · VOLUME 5
WRITTEN BY: KC

RACE O RAMA · NIGHT SKYLINE LENTICULAR SERIES
MATTEL DISNEY PIXAR CARS · VOLUME 6
WRITTEN BY: KC

EXPANDED UNIVERSE
MATTEL DISNEY PIXAR DIECAST CARS
TOONS · STORYTELLERS · DISNEY

ULTRA COMPLETIST
MATTEL DISNEY PIXAR CARS · 2005 THROUGH 2011
ULTRA COMPLETIST CHECKLIST

CARS 2 PORTO CORSA SERIES
MATTEL DISNEY PIXAR CARS 2 · VOLUME 9
WRITTEN BY: KC

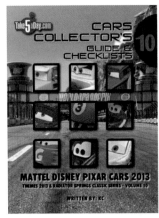

MATTEL DISNEY PIXAR CARS 2013
THEMES 2013 & RADIATOR SPRINGS CLASSIC SERIES · VOLUME 10
WRITTEN BY: KC

MATTEL DISNEY PIXAR CARS 2014
THEMES 2014, RS CLASSICS & TOONS · VOLUME 11
WRITTEN BY: KC

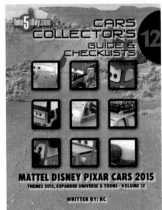

MATTEL DISNEY PIXAR CARS 2015
THEMES 2015, EXPANDED UNIVERSE & TOONS · VOLUME 12
WRITTEN BY: KC

MATTEL DISNEY PIXAR CARS 2016
THEMES 2016, RS CLASSICS, PRECISION SERIES & EXPANDED UNIVERSE
WRITTEN BY: KC

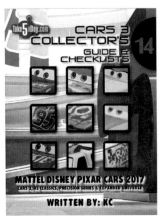

MATTEL DISNEY PIXAR CARS 2017
CARS 3, RS CLASSICS, PRECISION SERIES & EXPANDED UNIVERSE
WRITTEN BY: KC

THE COMPLETE OPEN CHECKLIST
MATTEL DISNEY PLANES & PLANES FIRE & RESCUE
EVERYTHING FROM DIECAST 2013 TO 2016
WRITTEN BY: KC

**COMPLETE CARS 1 ONLY
YEAR BY YEAR OPEN CHECKLIST**
MATTEL DISNEY PIXAR CARS · 2006 THROUGH 2016
WRITTEN BY: KC

Worldwide Ordering Now available through the TakeFiveADay.com Magcloud link or http://bit.ly/t5store.

Made in the USA
Columbia, SC
13 January 2021